AF575468

ART NOUVEAU

Objects and Artifacts

ART NOUVEAU

Objects and Artifacts

ANTON SEDER

DOVER PUBLICATIONS
Garden City, New York

Bibliographical Note

Art Nouveau: Objects and Artifacts, first published by Dover Publications in 2015, is a republication of *Esquisses d'art industriel: métal, céramique, verre,* originally published by Henri Laurens [Editeur], Paris, [1899?]. A Note has been provided specially for this edition.

DOVER *Pictorial Archive* SERIES

International Standard Book Number

ISBN-13: 978-0-486-79733-5
ISBN-10: 0-486-79733-3

Printed in Canada
79733304 2025
www.doverpublications.com

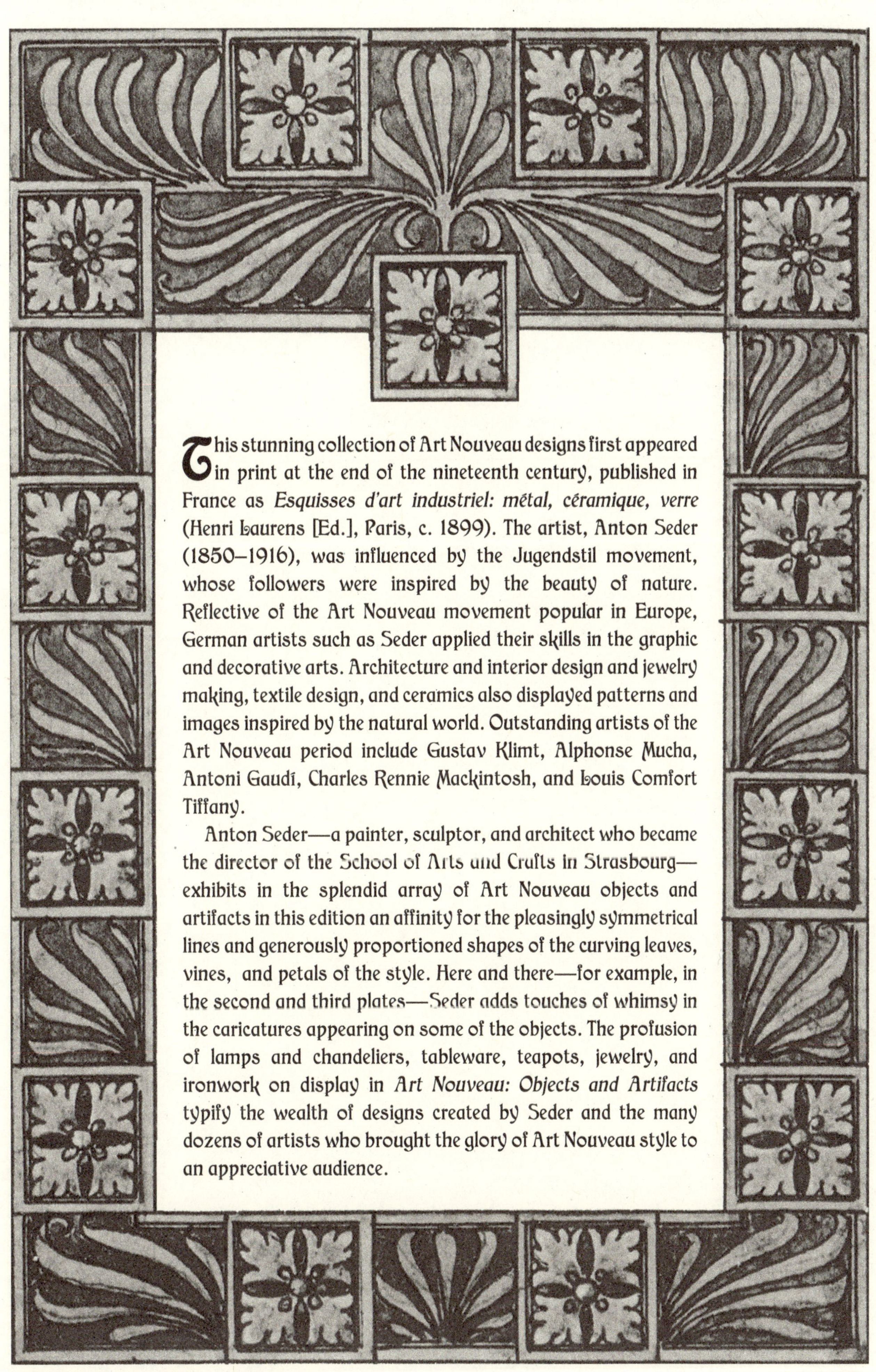

This stunning collection of Art Nouveau designs first appeared in print at the end of the nineteenth century, published in France as *Esquisses d'art industriel: métal, céramique, verre* (Henri Laurens [Ed.], Paris, c. 1899). The artist, Anton Seder (1850–1916), was influenced by the Jugendstil movement, whose followers were inspired by the beauty of nature. Reflective of the Art Nouveau movement popular in Europe, German artists such as Seder applied their skills in the graphic and decorative arts. Architecture and interior design and jewelry making, textile design, and ceramics also displayed patterns and images inspired by the natural world. Outstanding artists of the Art Nouveau period include Gustav Klimt, Alphonse Mucha, Antoni Gaudí, Charles Rennie Mackintosh, and Louis Comfort Tiffany.

Anton Seder—a painter, sculptor, and architect who became the director of the School of Arts and Crafts in Strasbourg—exhibits in the splendid array of Art Nouveau objects and artifacts in this edition an affinity for the pleasingly symmetrical lines and generously proportioned shapes of the curving leaves, vines, and petals of the style. Here and there—for example, in the second and third plates—Seder adds touches of whimsy in the caricatures appearing on some of the objects. The profusion of lamps and chandeliers, tableware, teapots, jewelry, and ironwork on display in *Art Nouveau: Objects and Artifacts* typify the wealth of designs created by Seder and the many dozens of artists who brought the glory of Art Nouveau style to an appreciative audience.

ART NOUVEAU

Objects and Artifacts

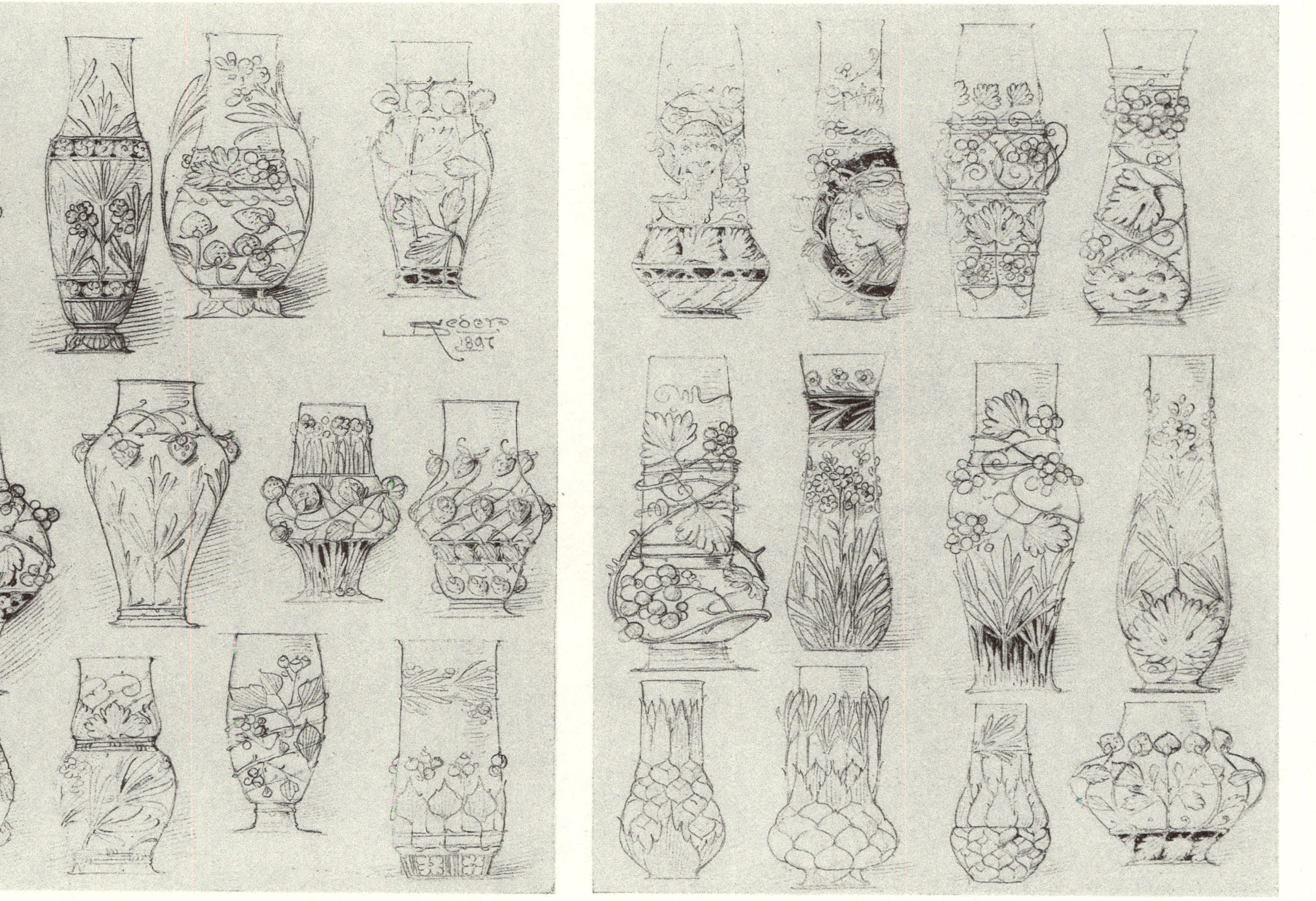
Weber
1897

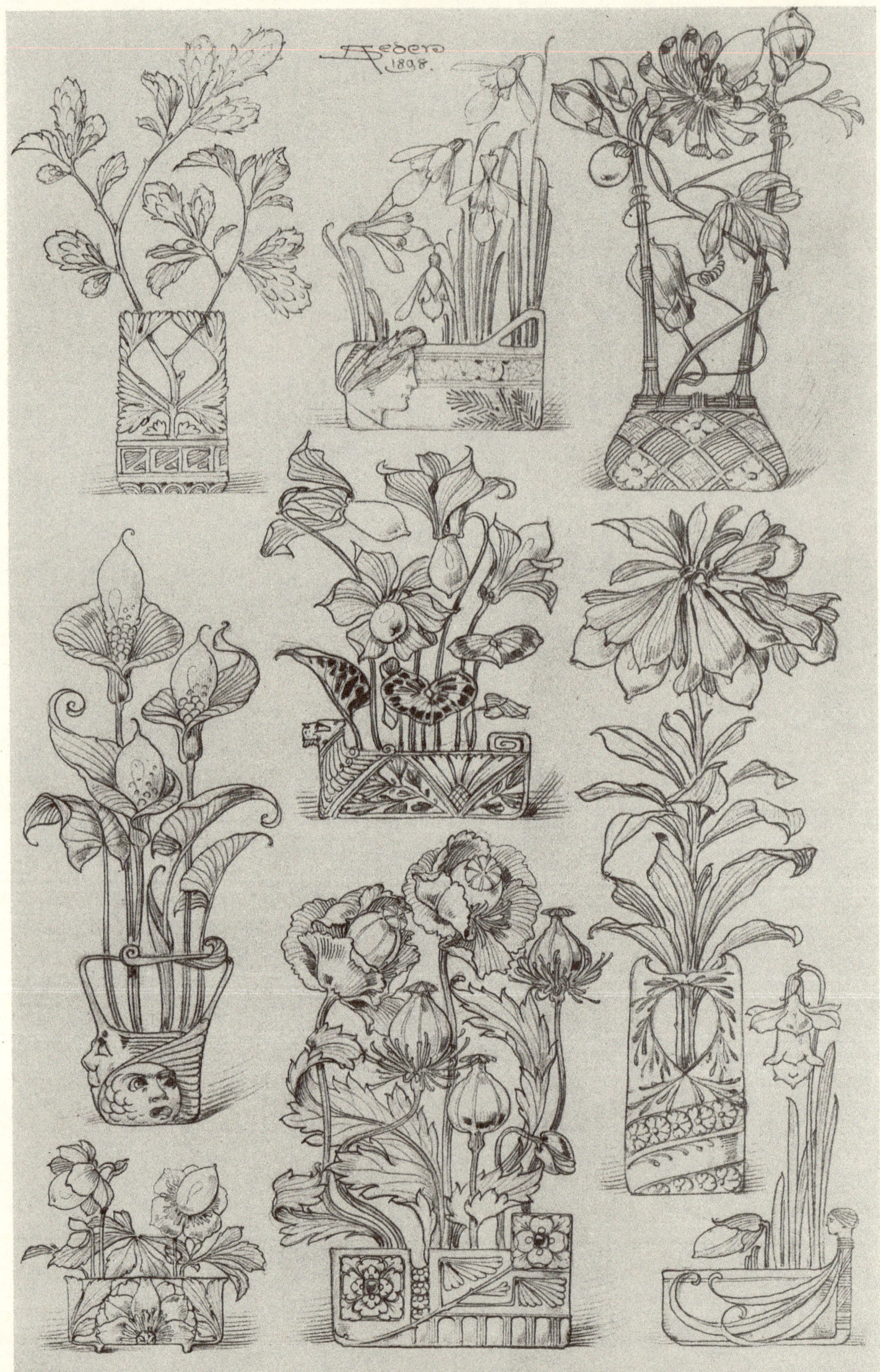
1898.

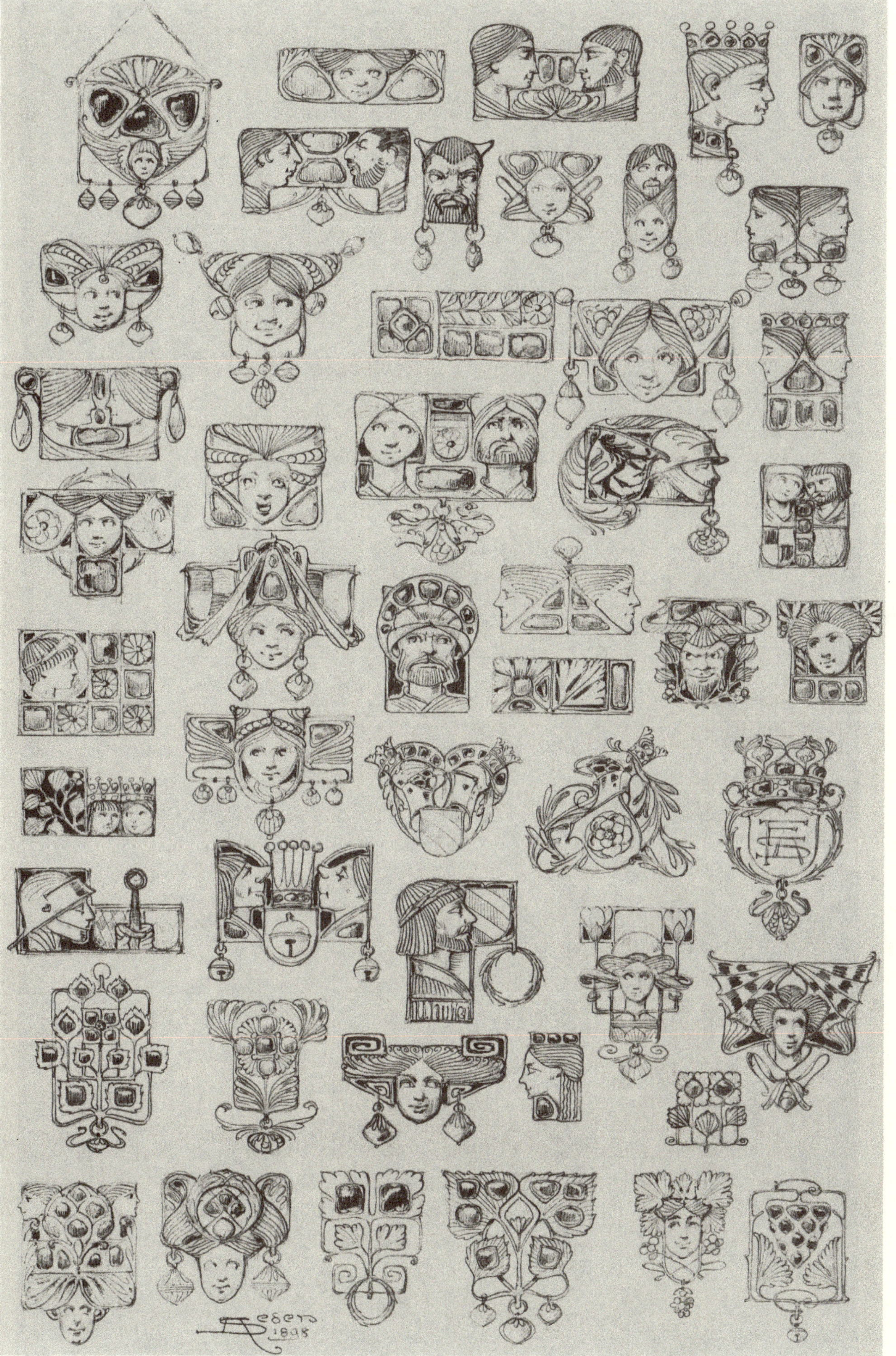
Seder
1898

1898

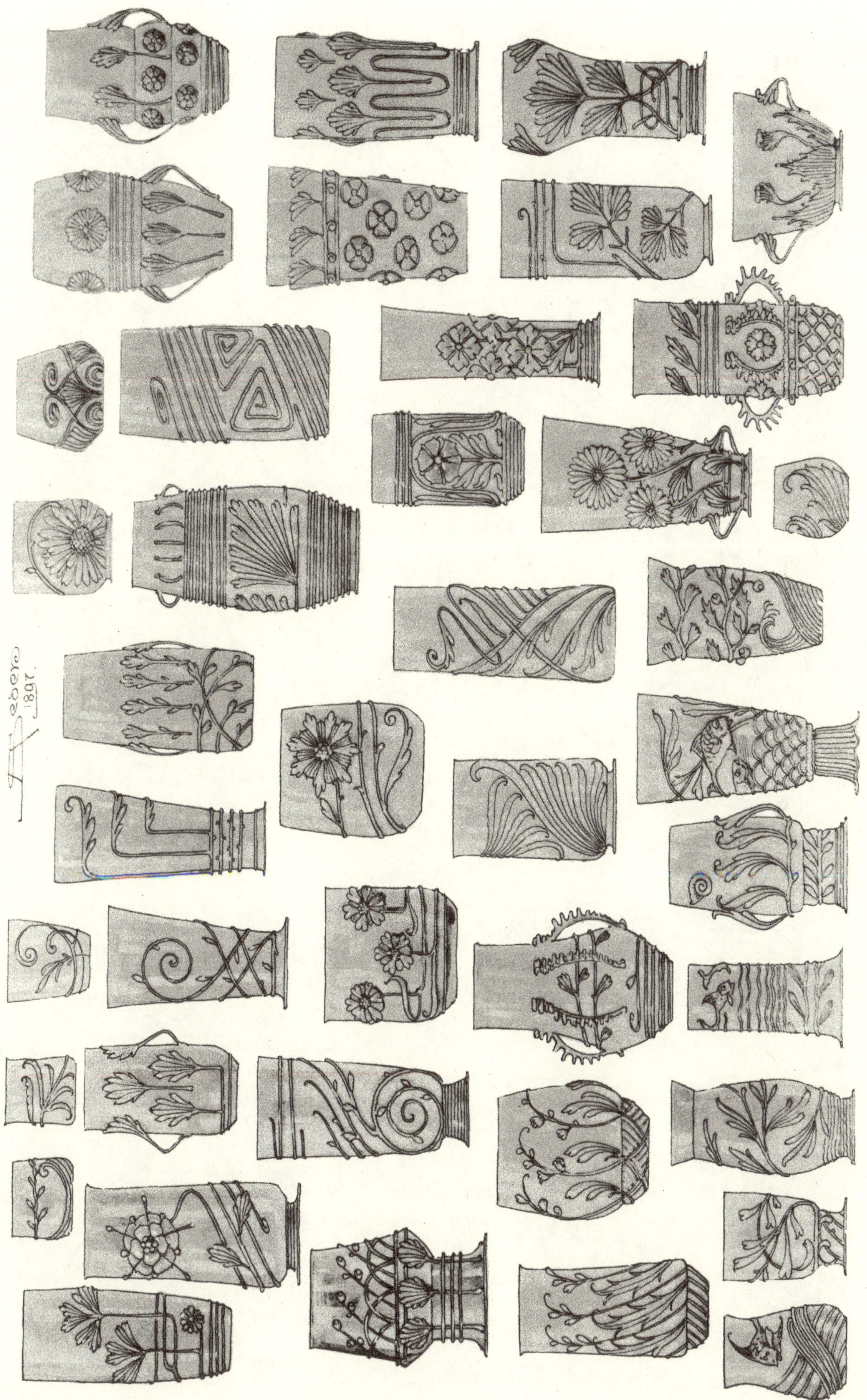

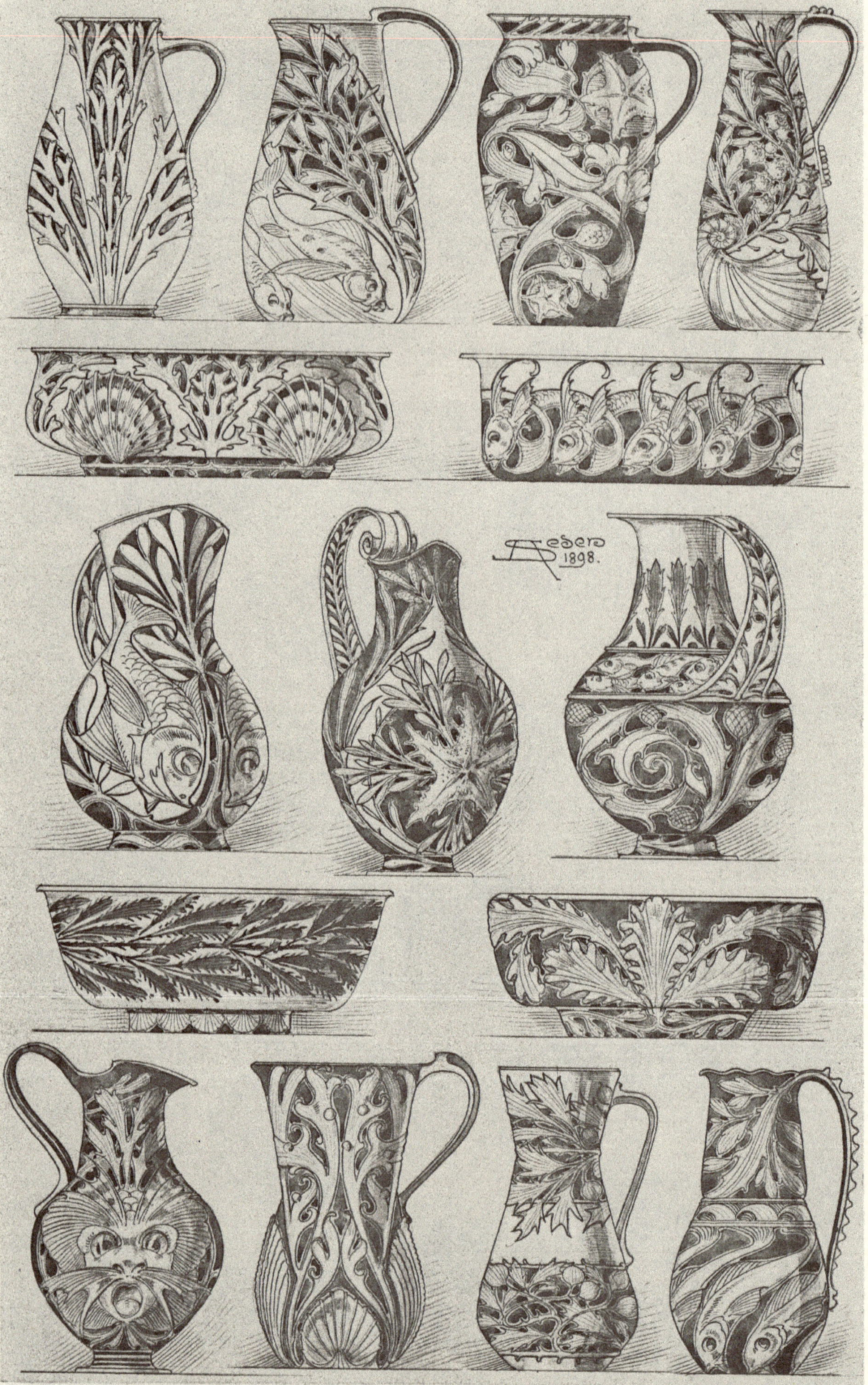
1898.

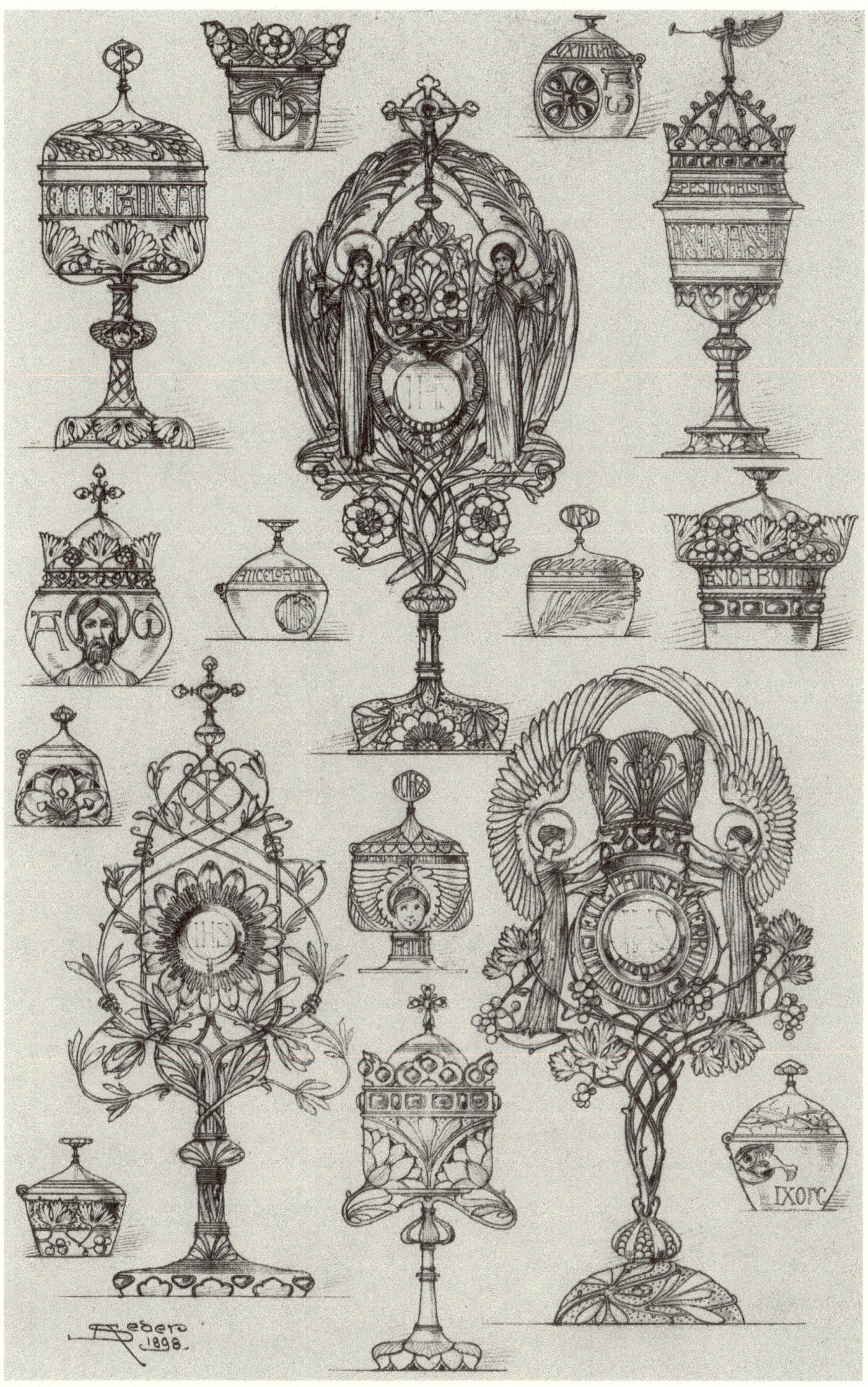
IHS
1898.

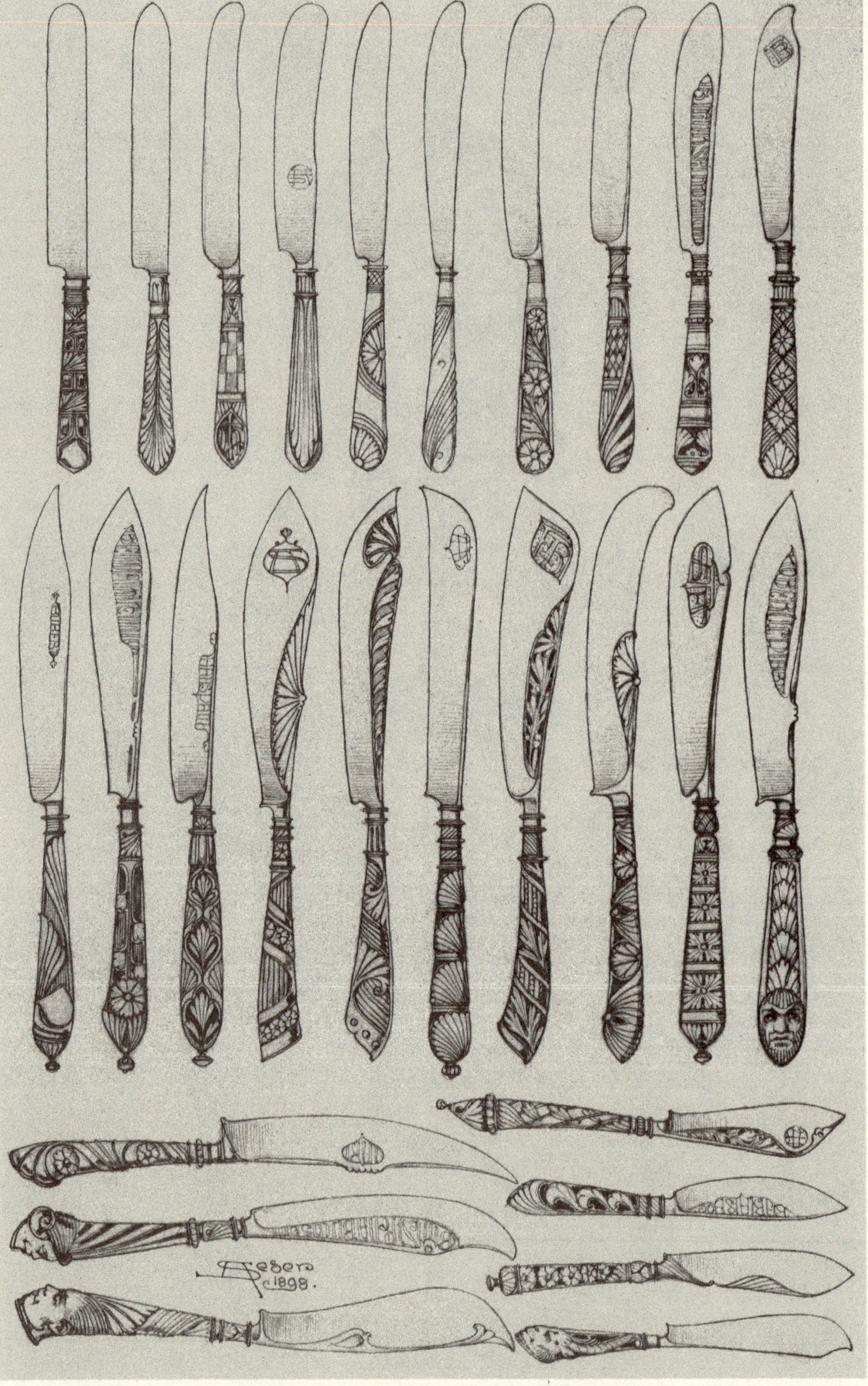
1898.

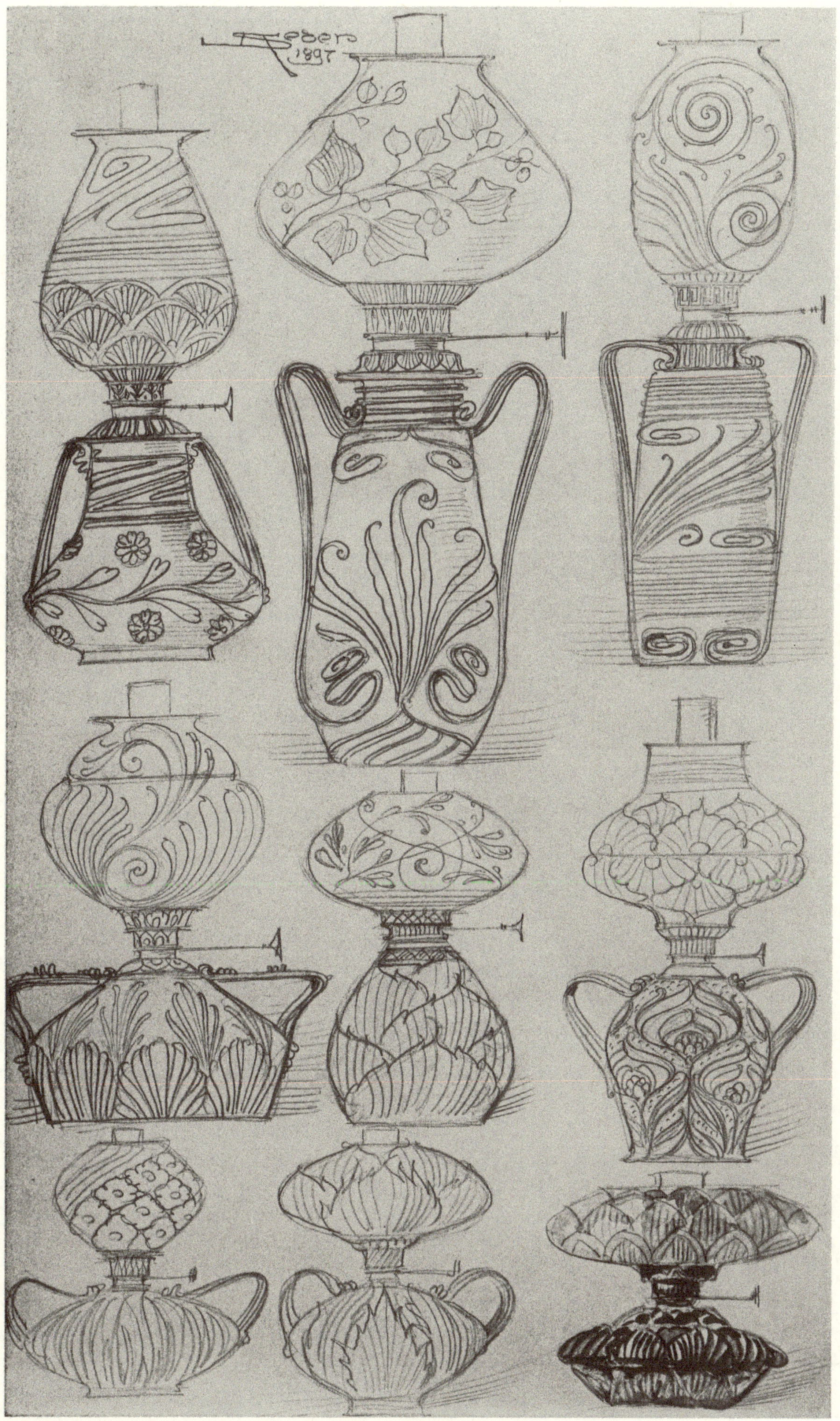

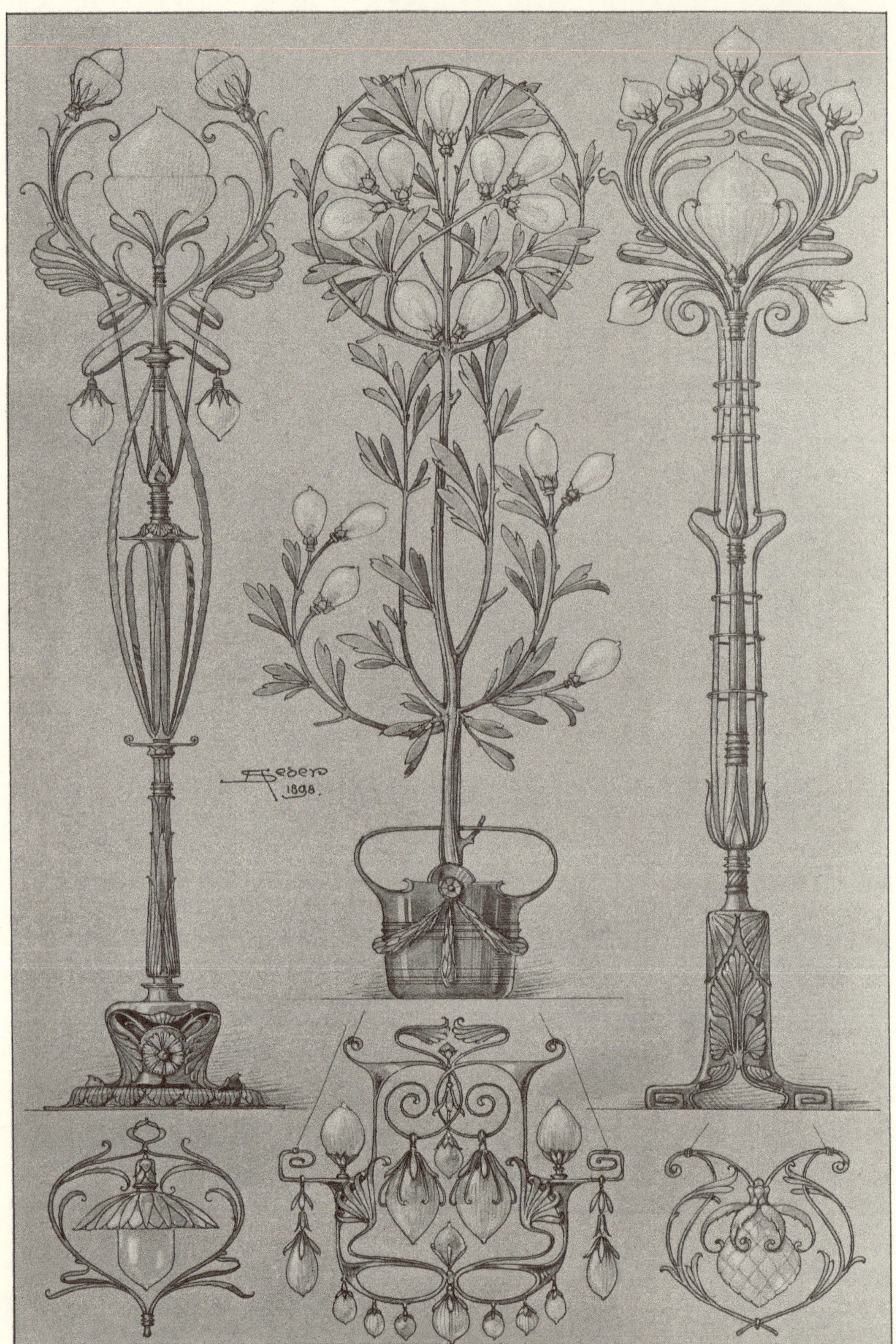
1898.

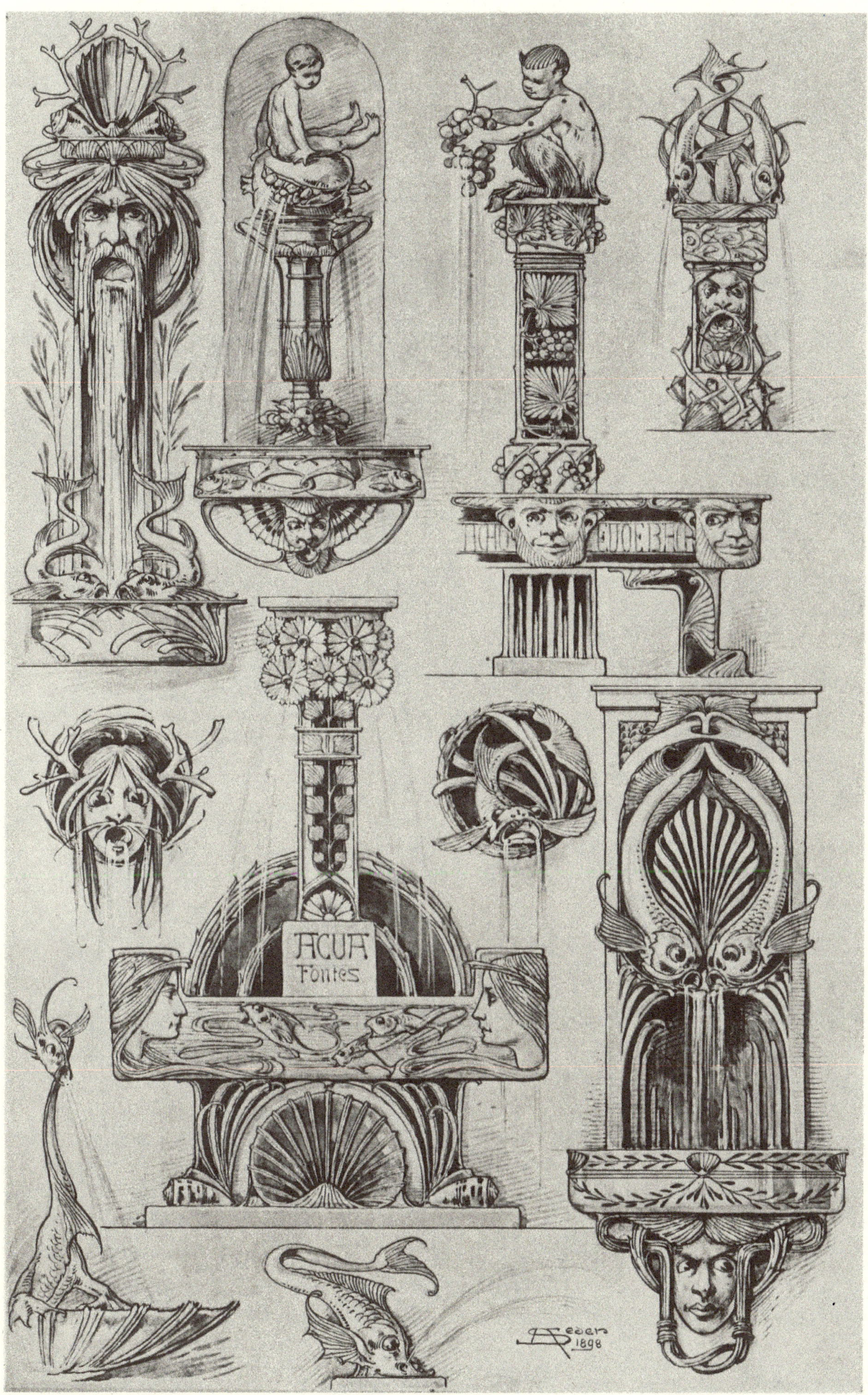
ACUA
Fontes
1898

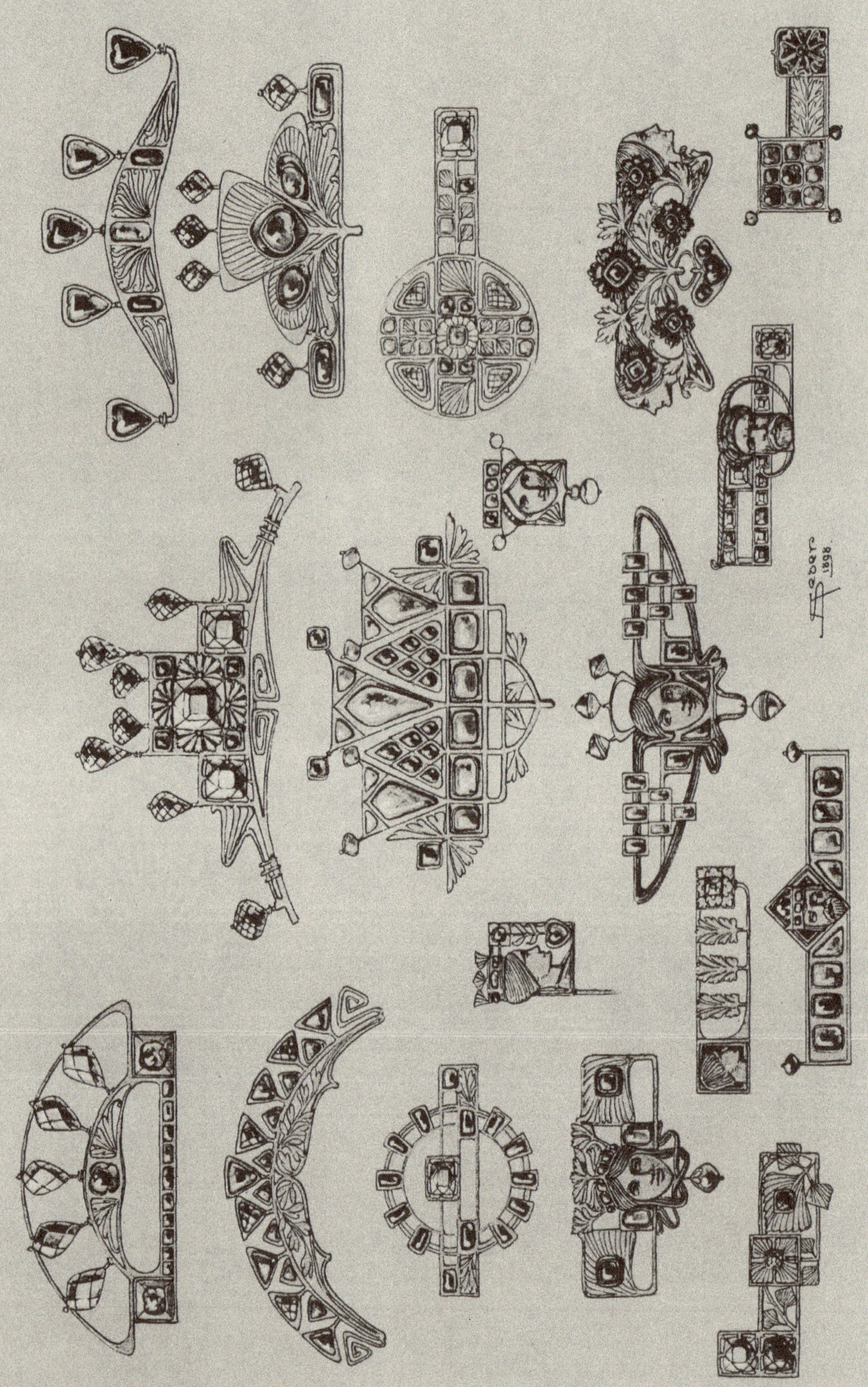

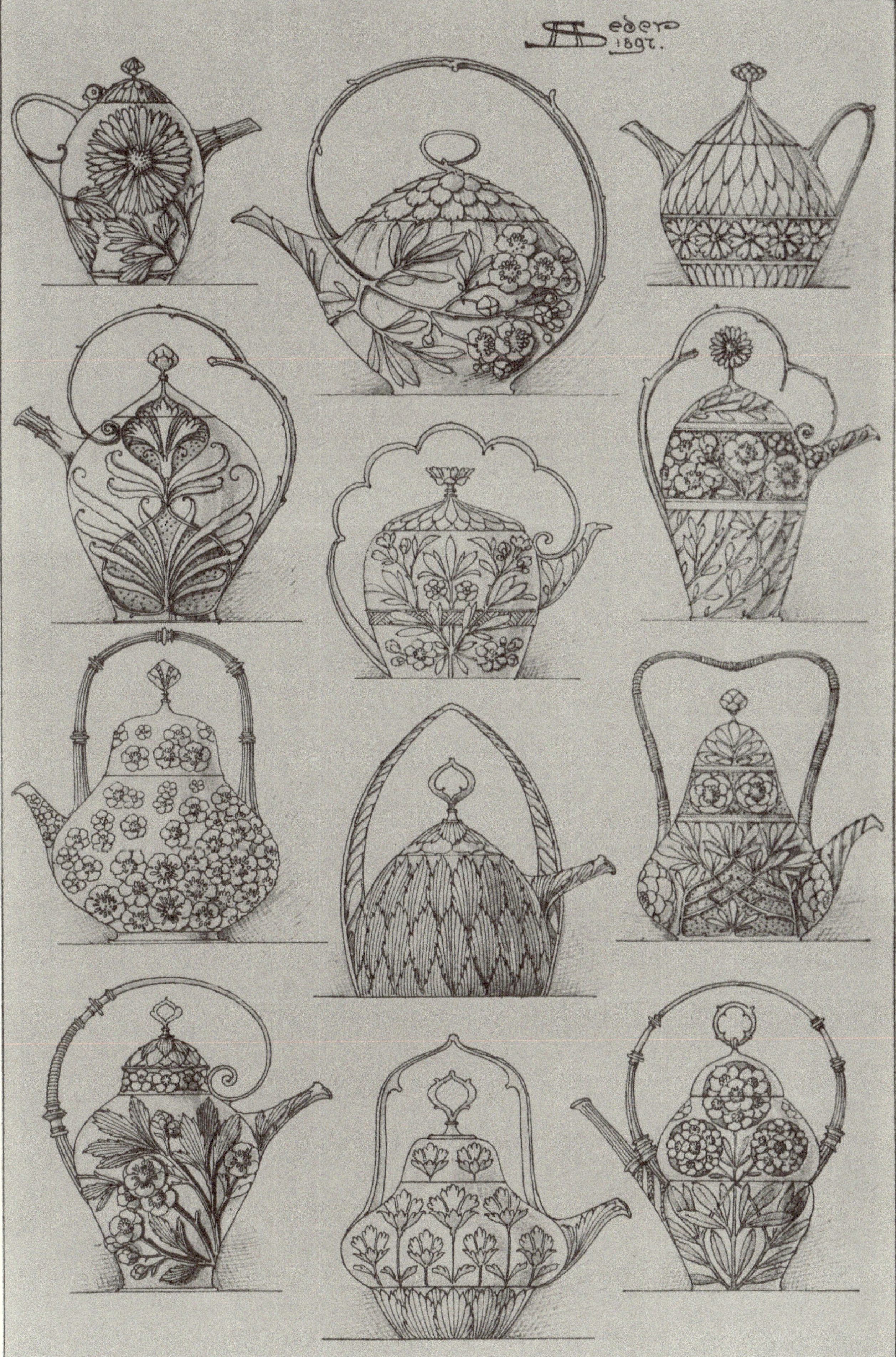
eder
1897.

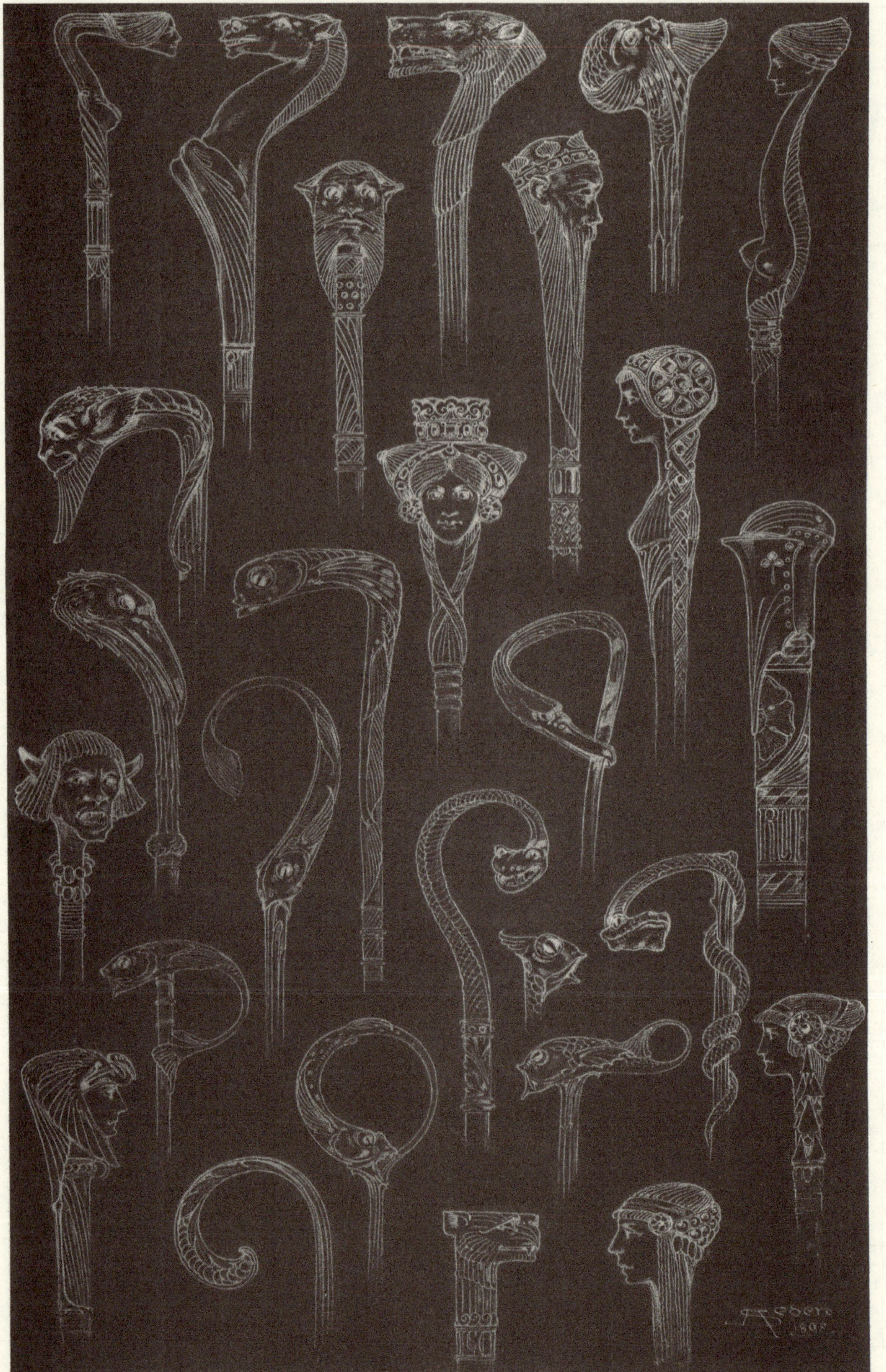

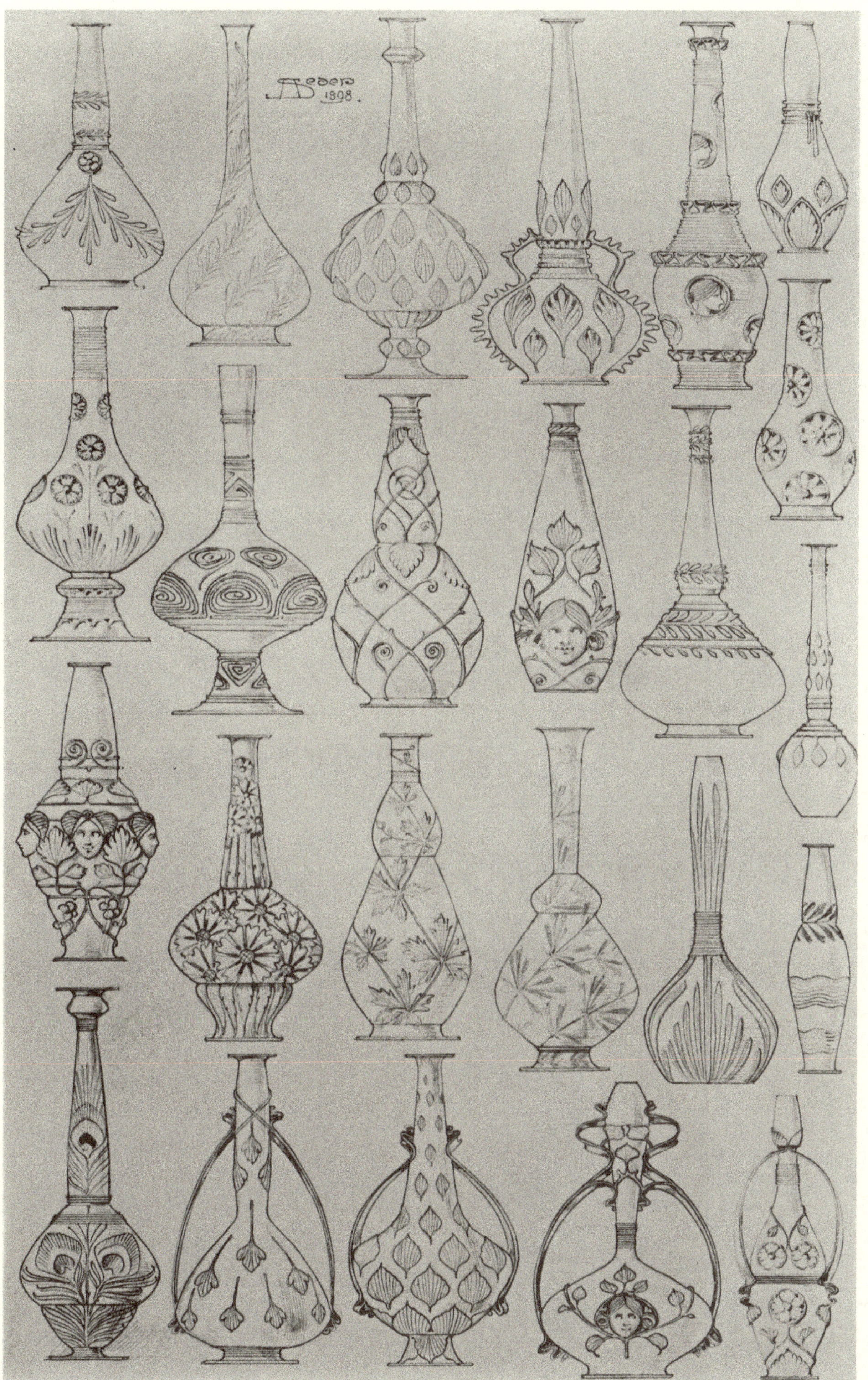
Seder
1898.

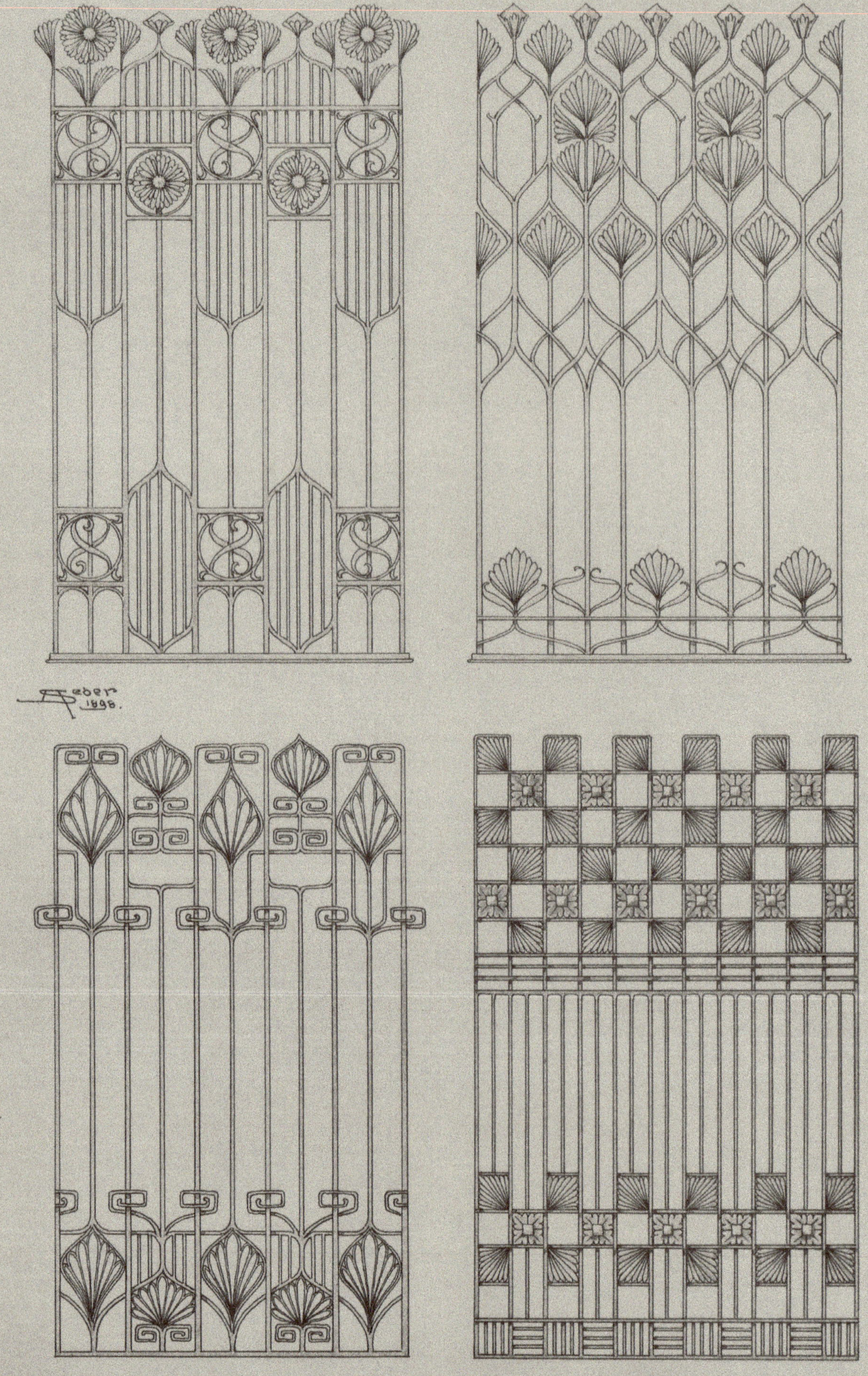
1898.

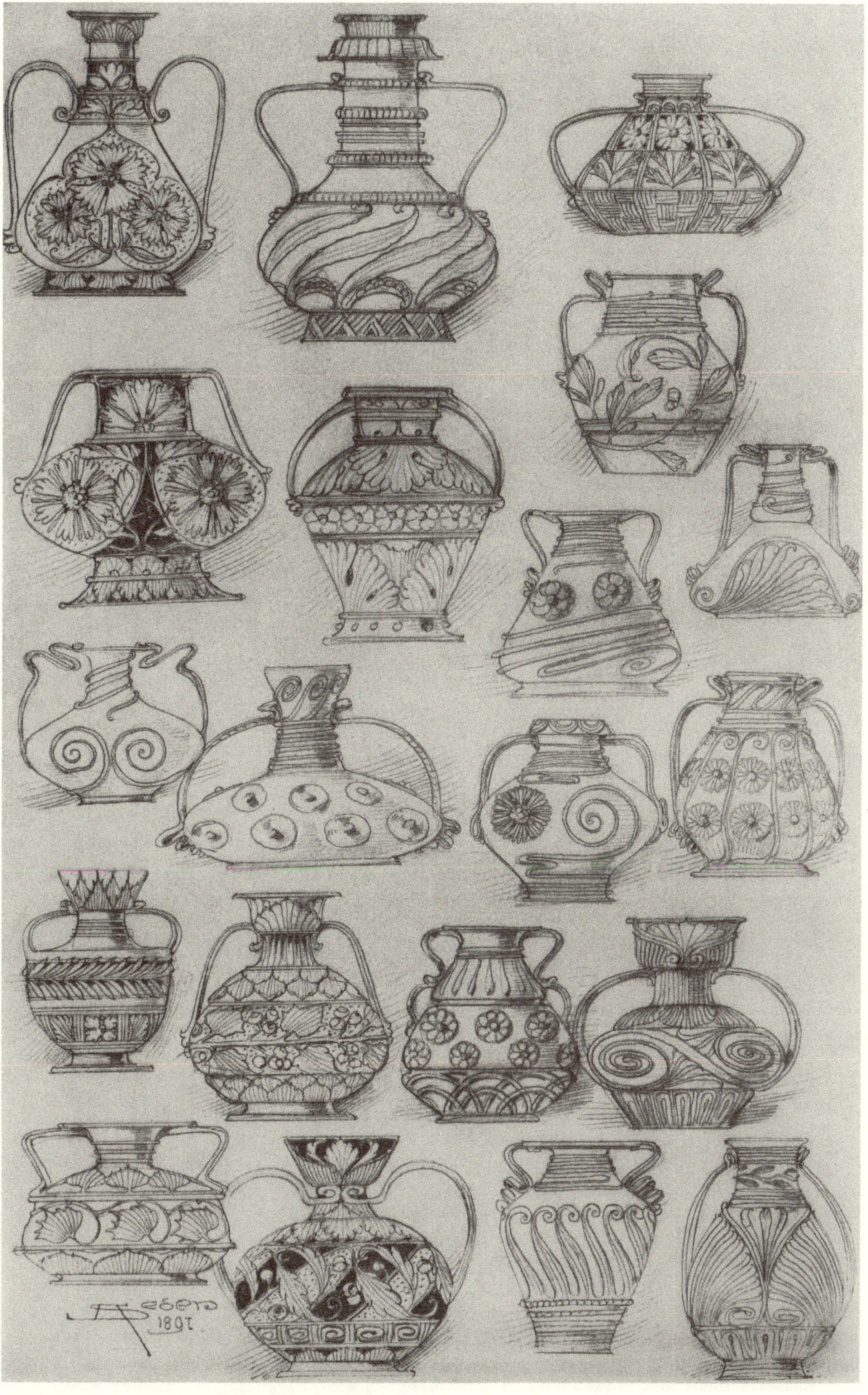
1897

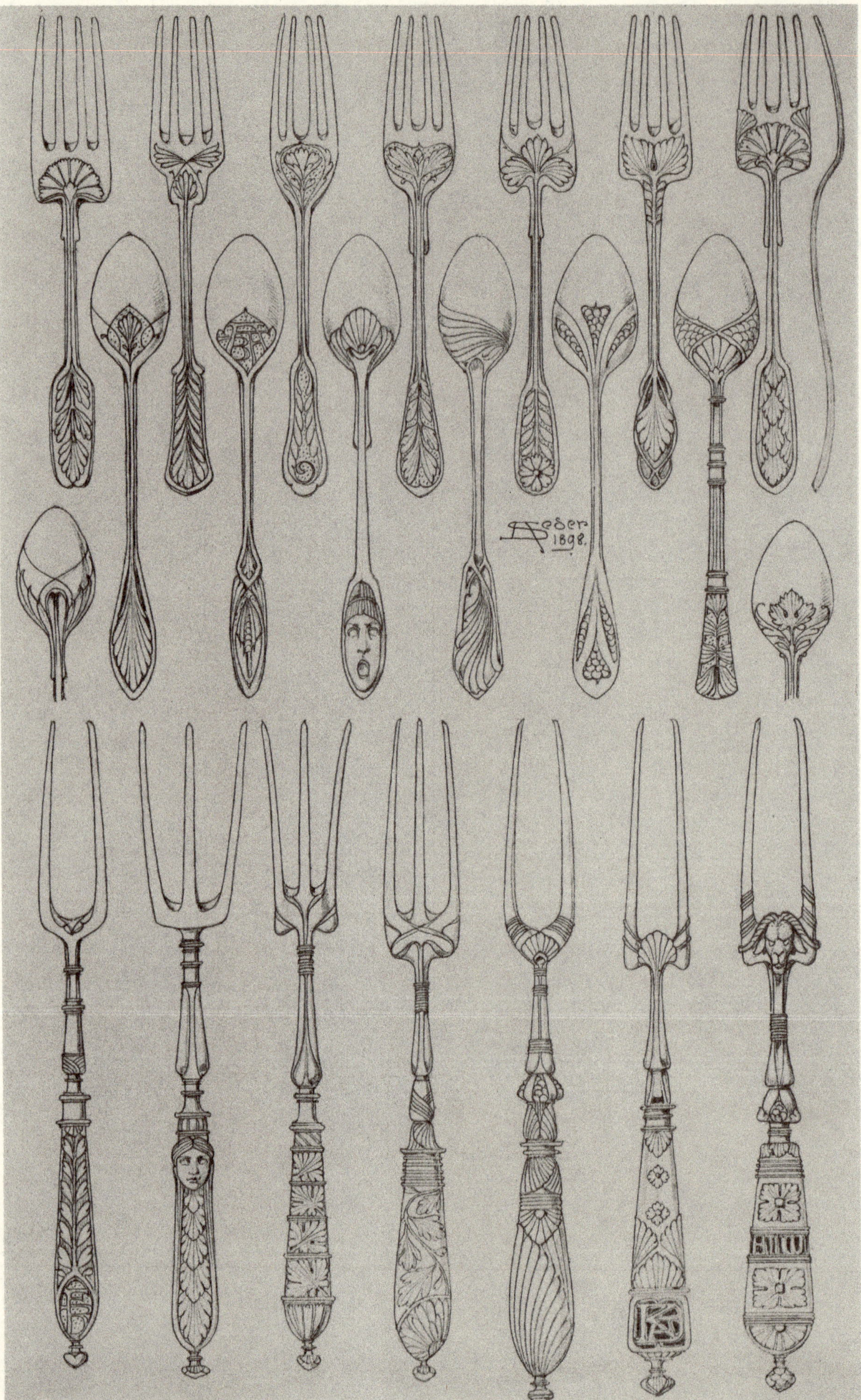
Seder
1898.

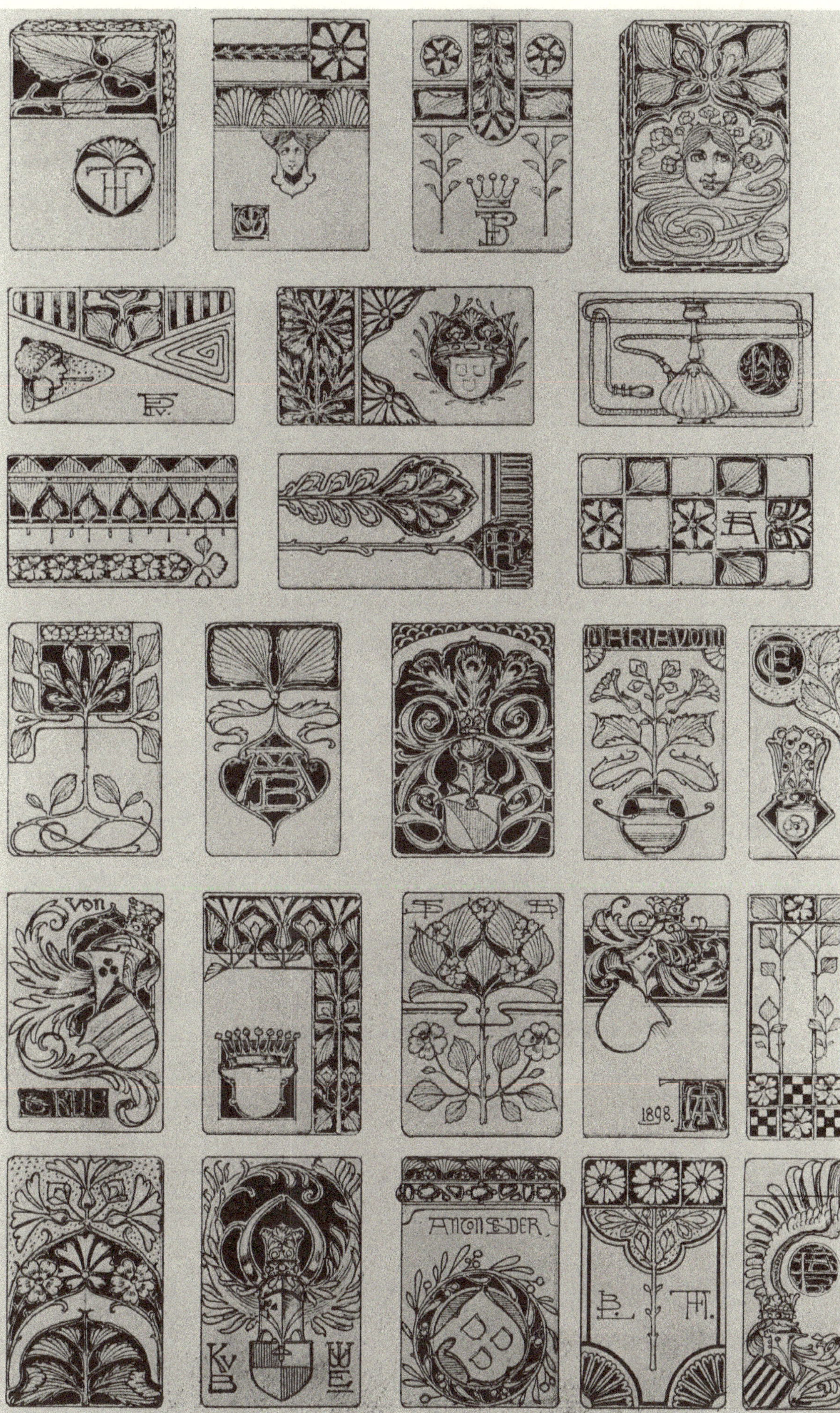

von
1898.
ANTON EDER

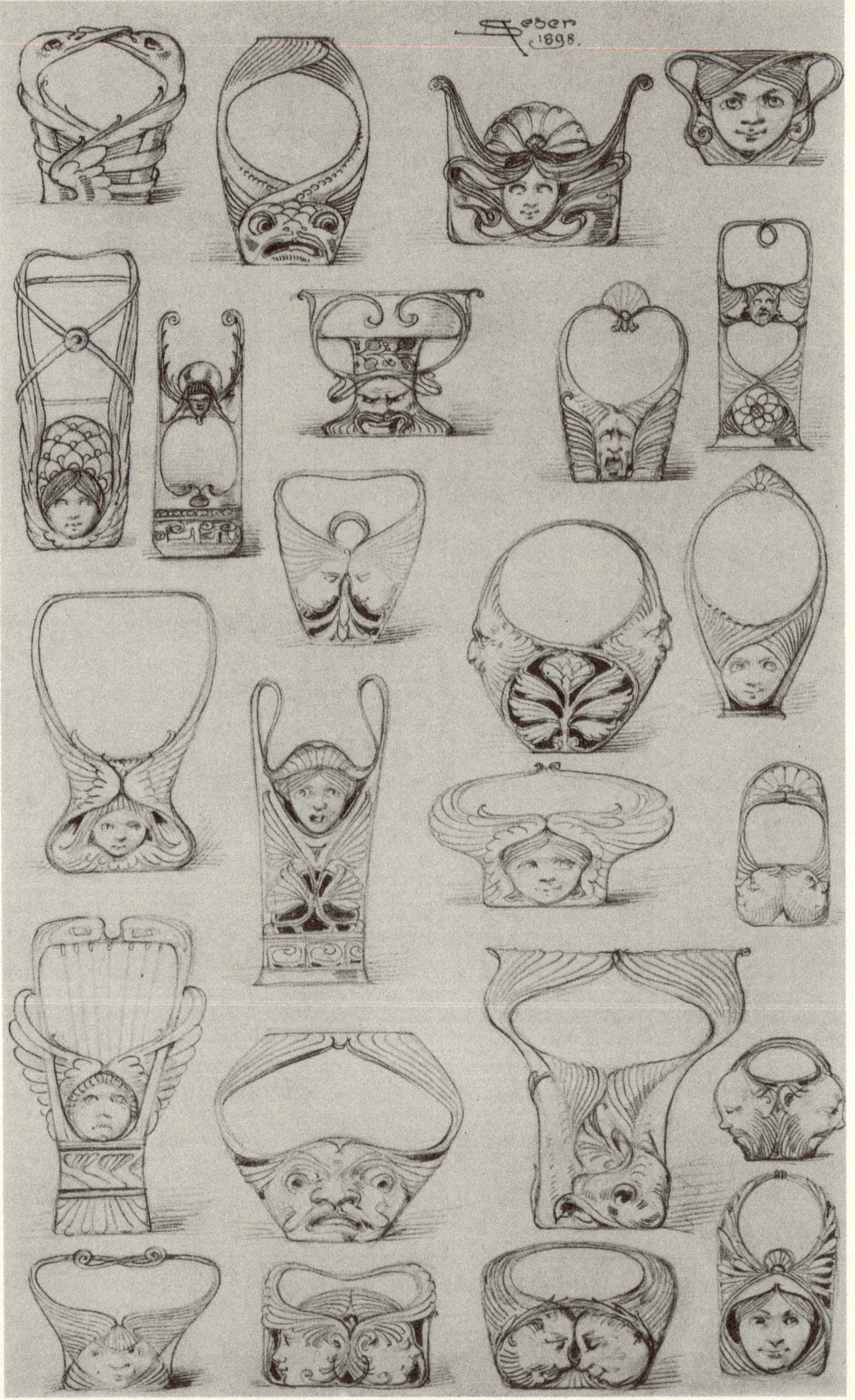
1898.

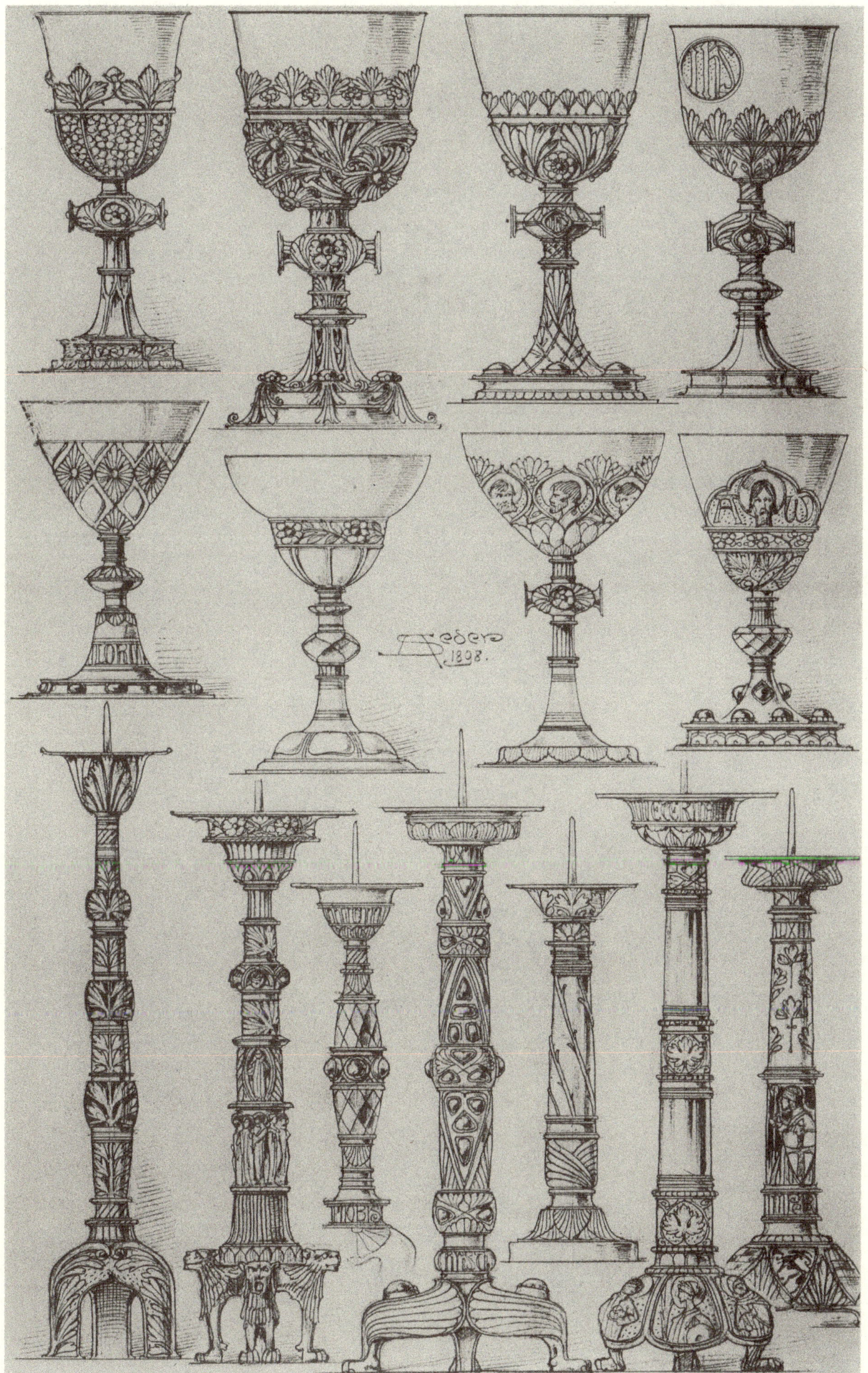
Seder
1898.

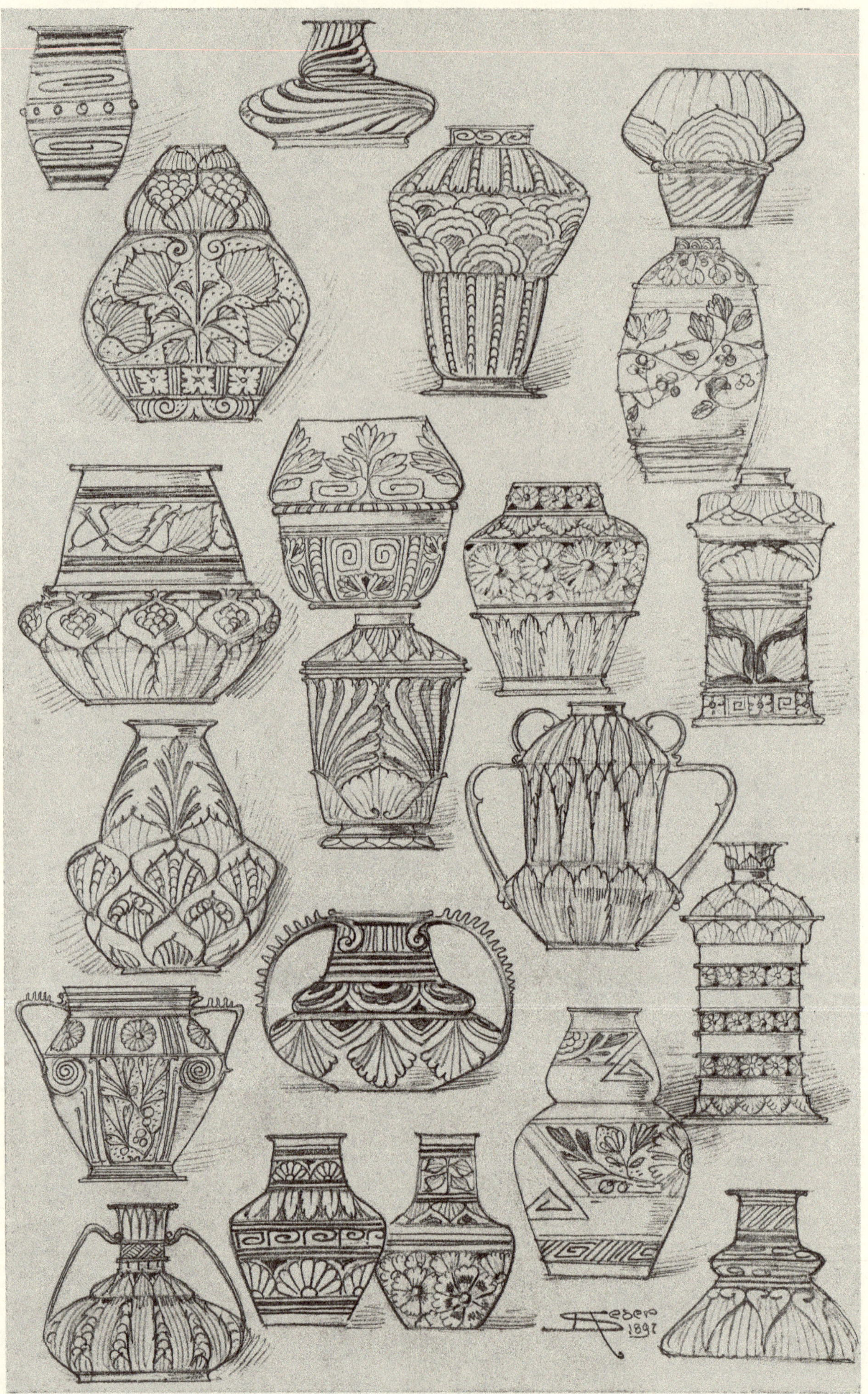
Seder
1897

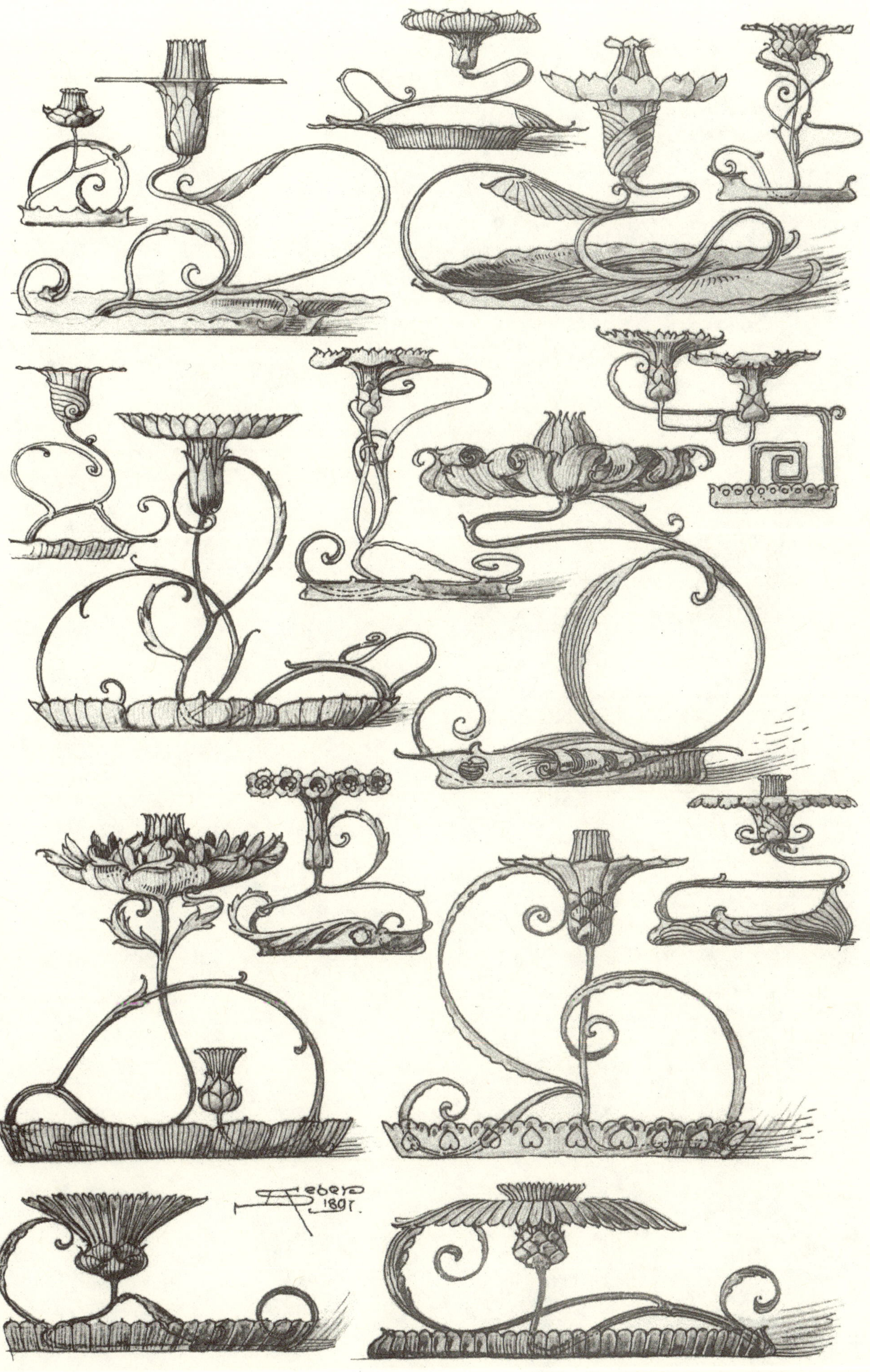

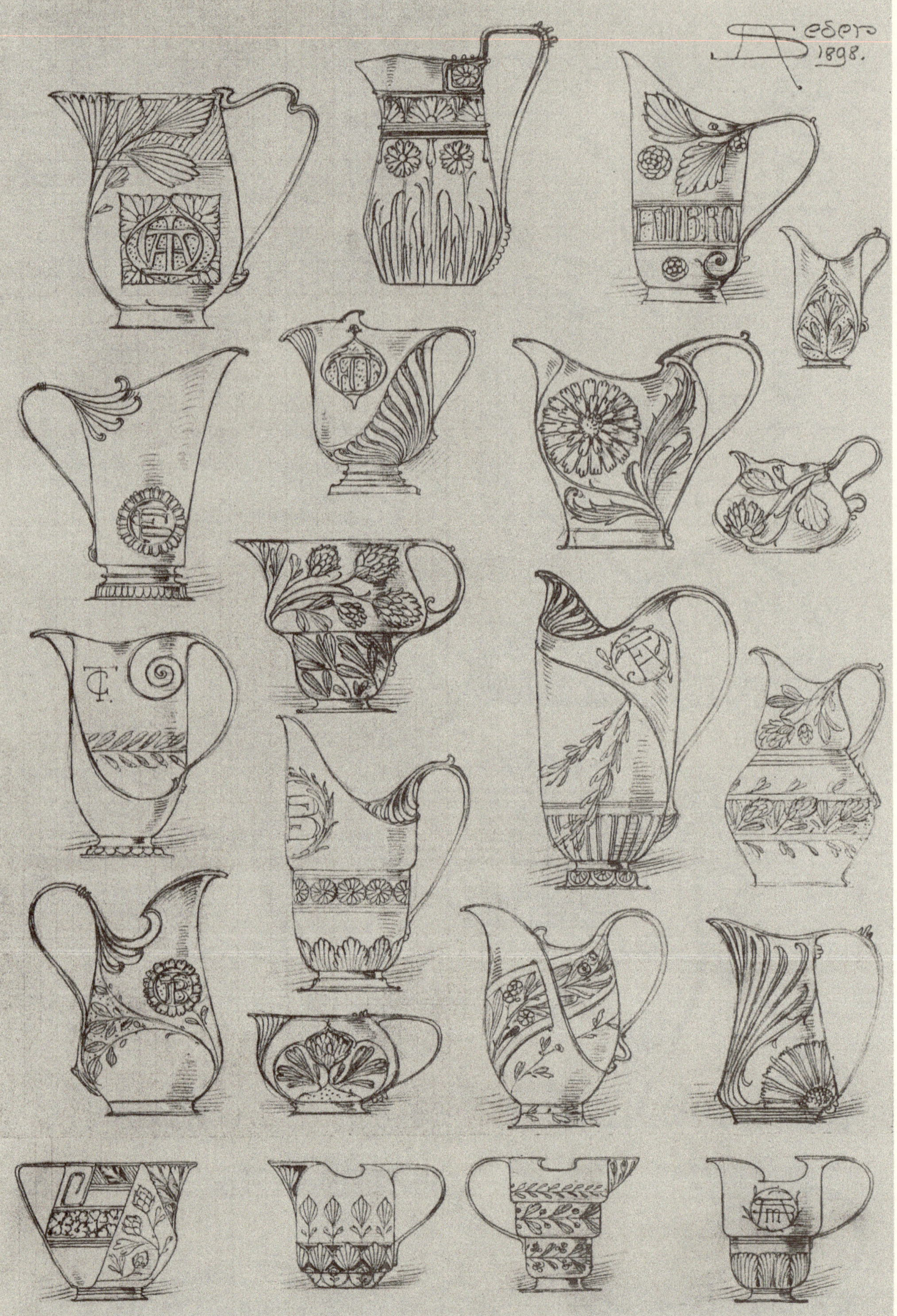
1898.

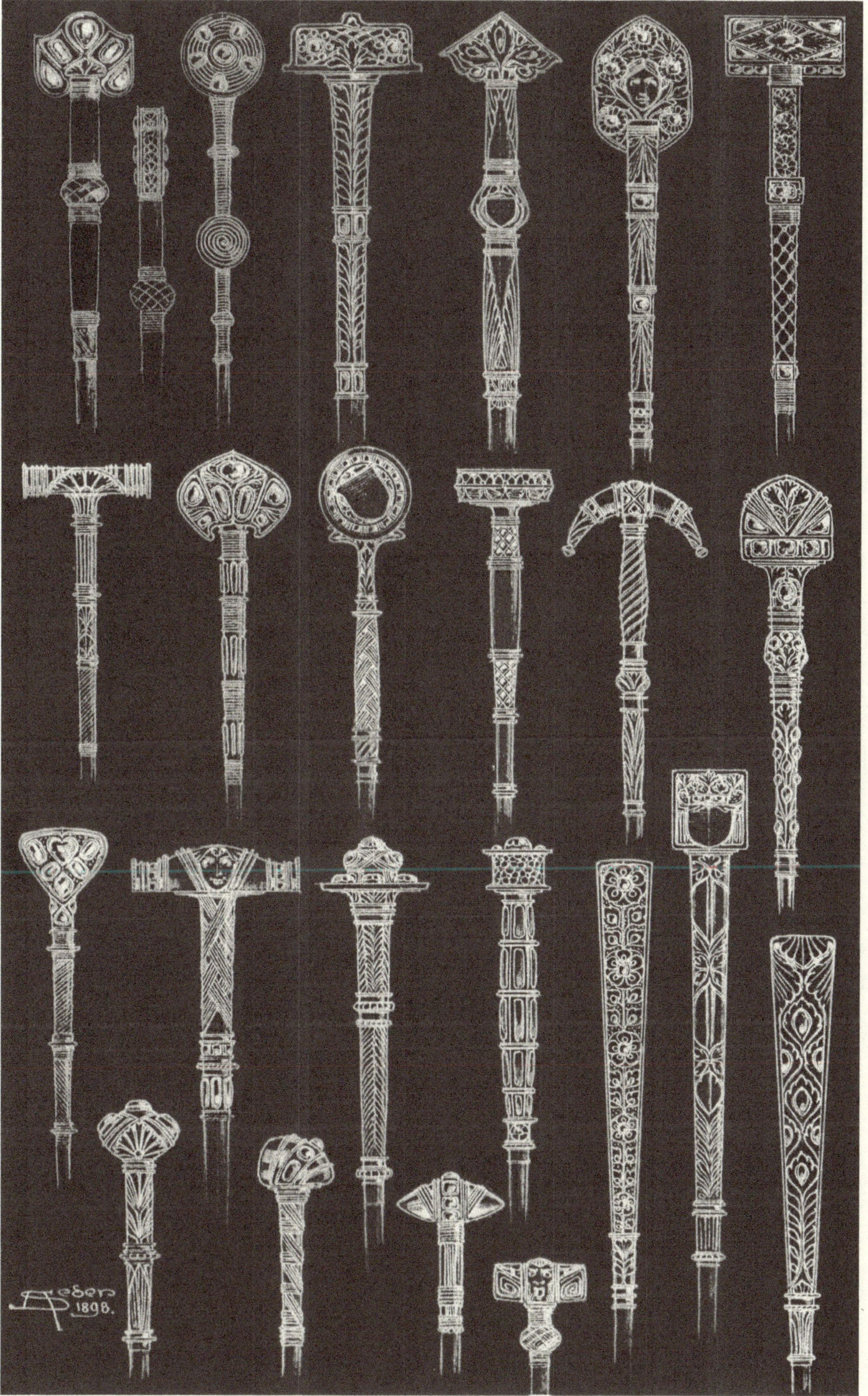
1898.

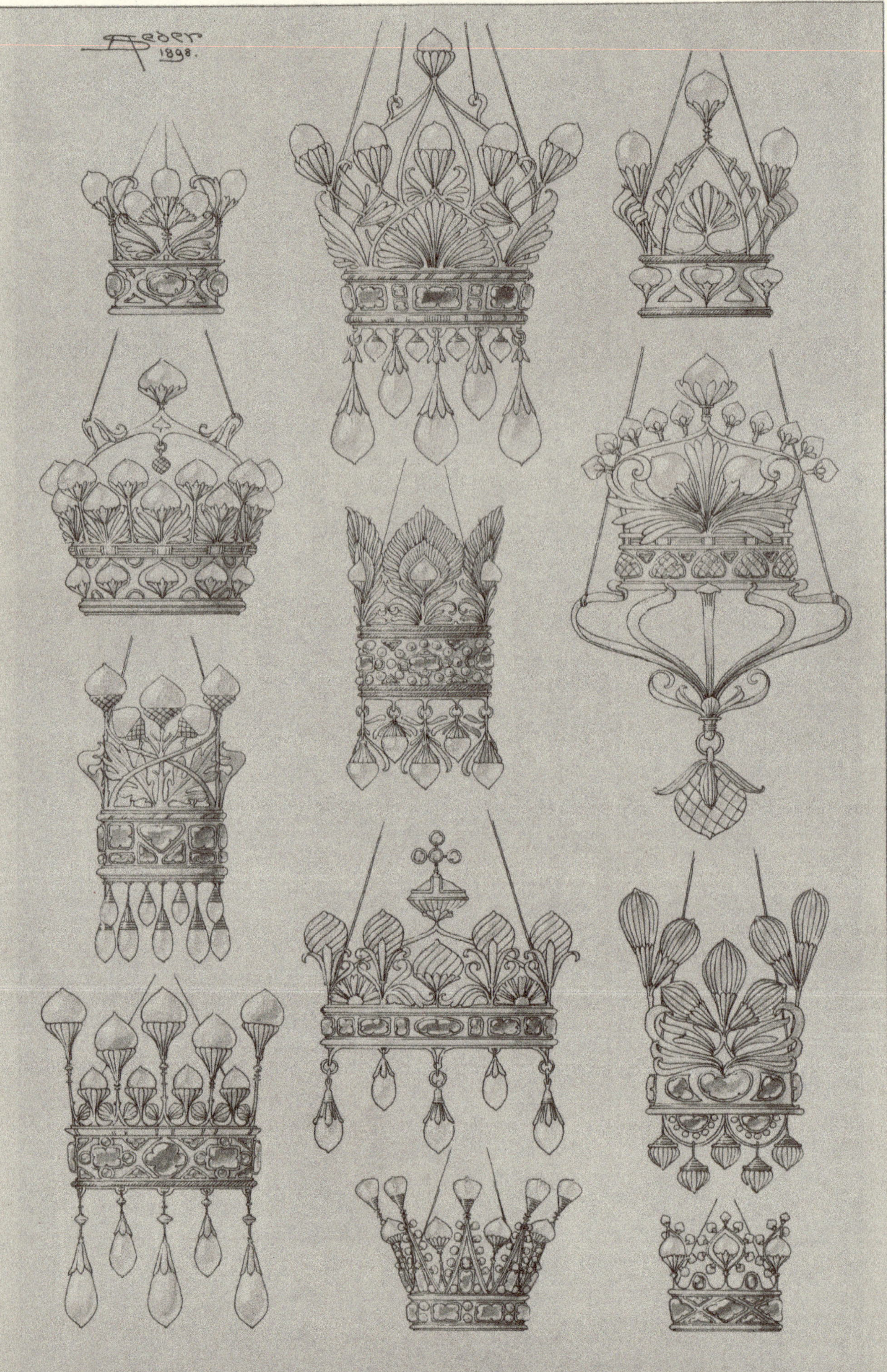
Seder
1898.

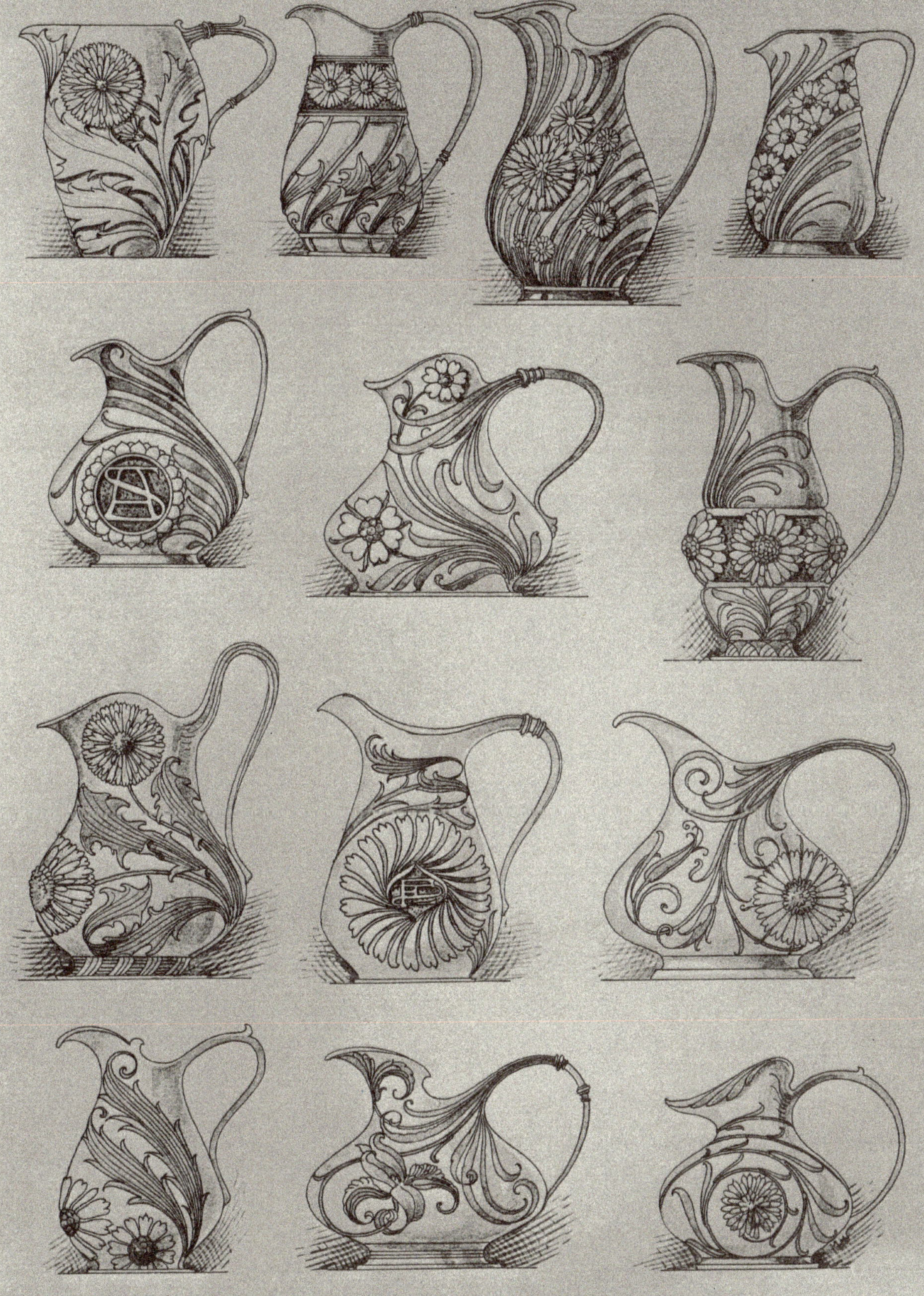
Seder
1897.

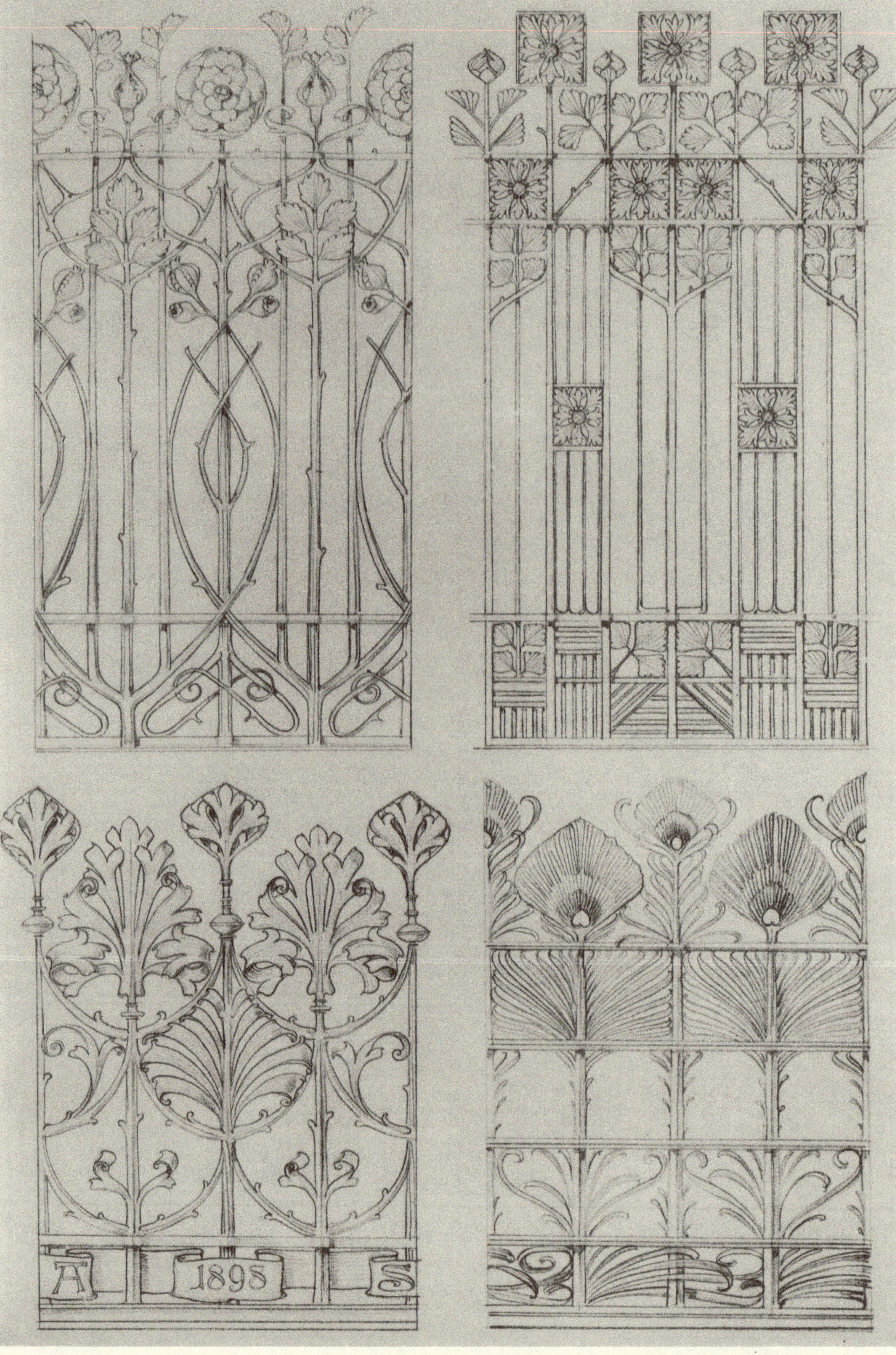
A
1898
S

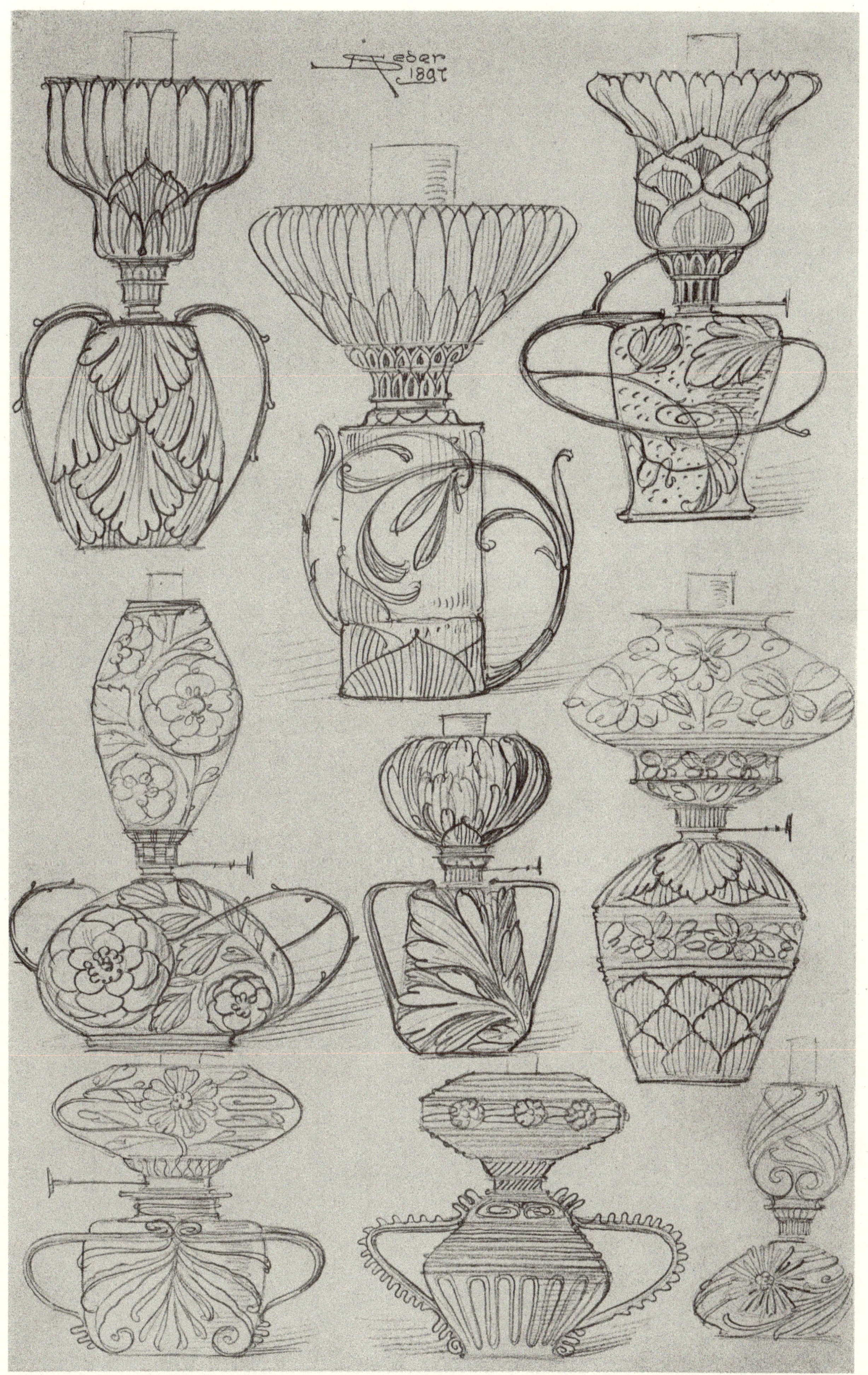
1897

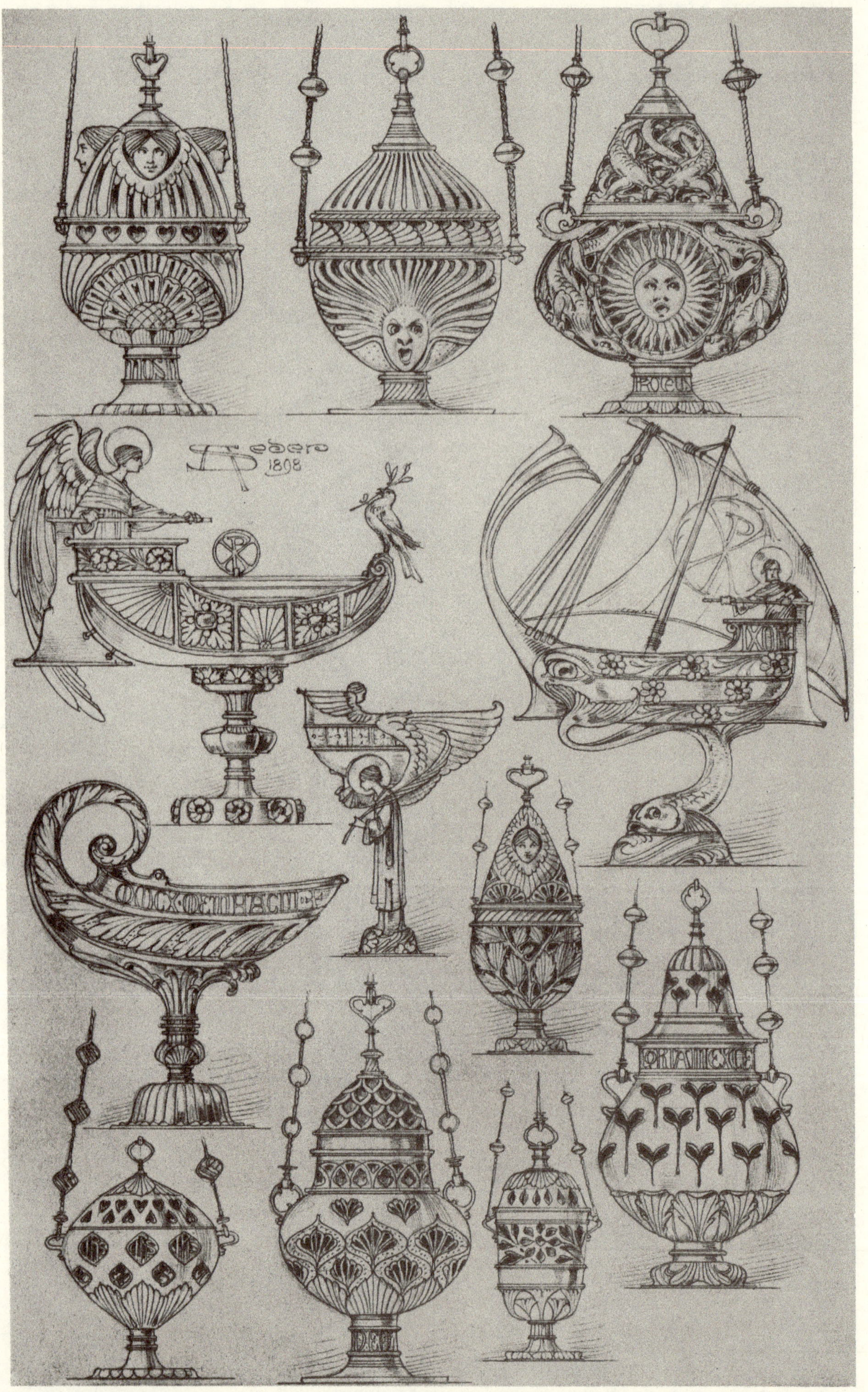

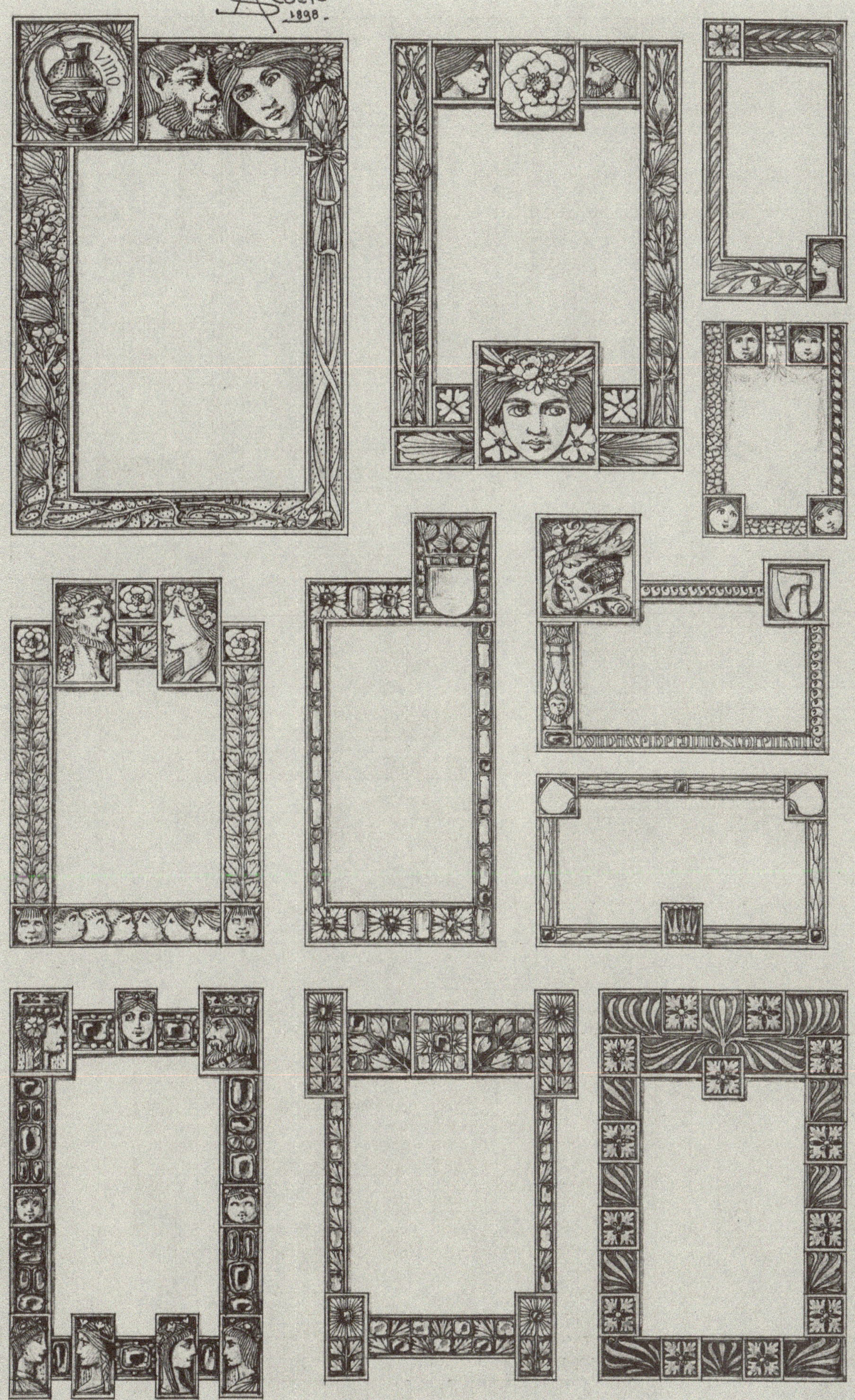

Seder
1898
VINO

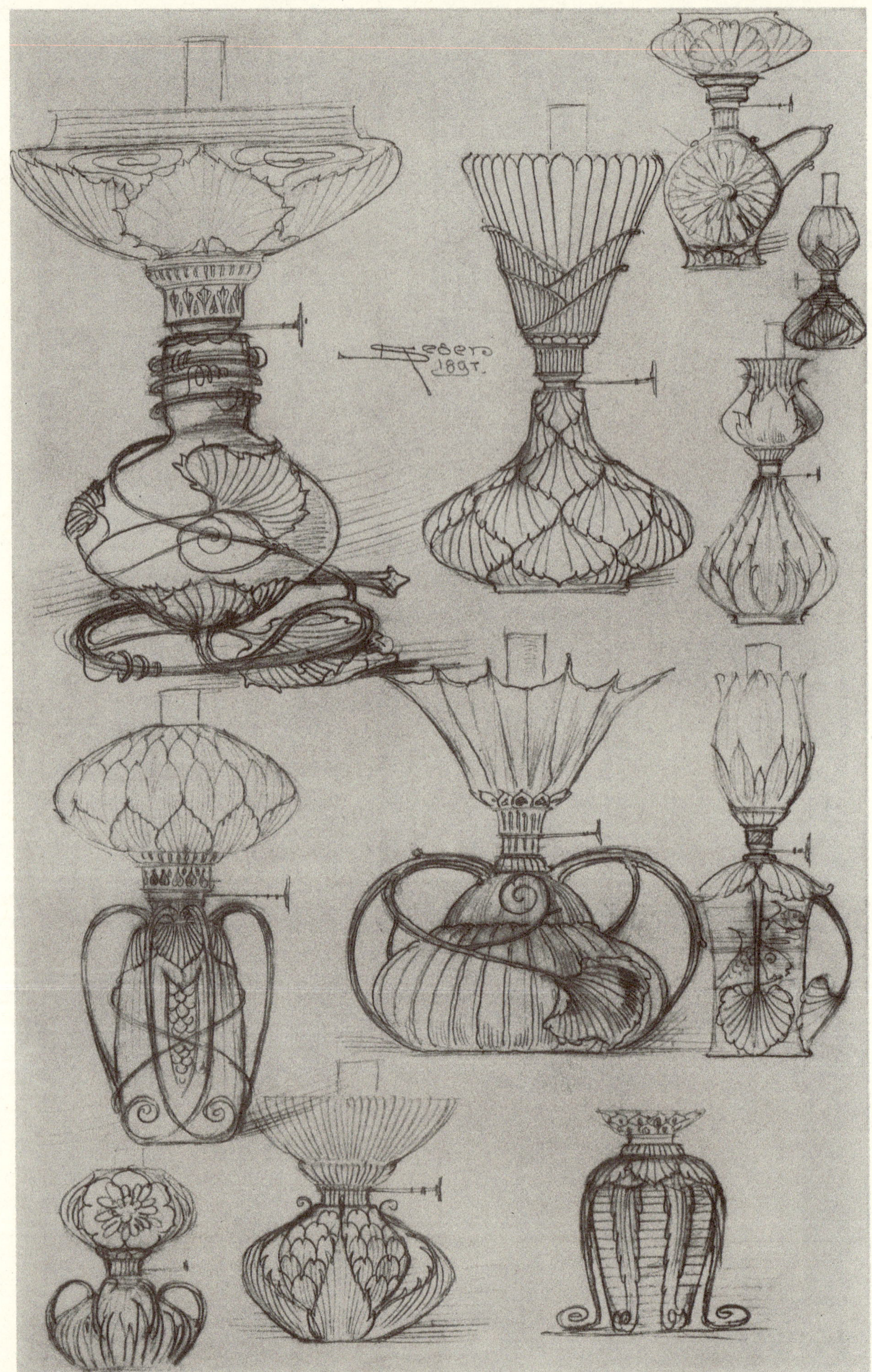
1897.

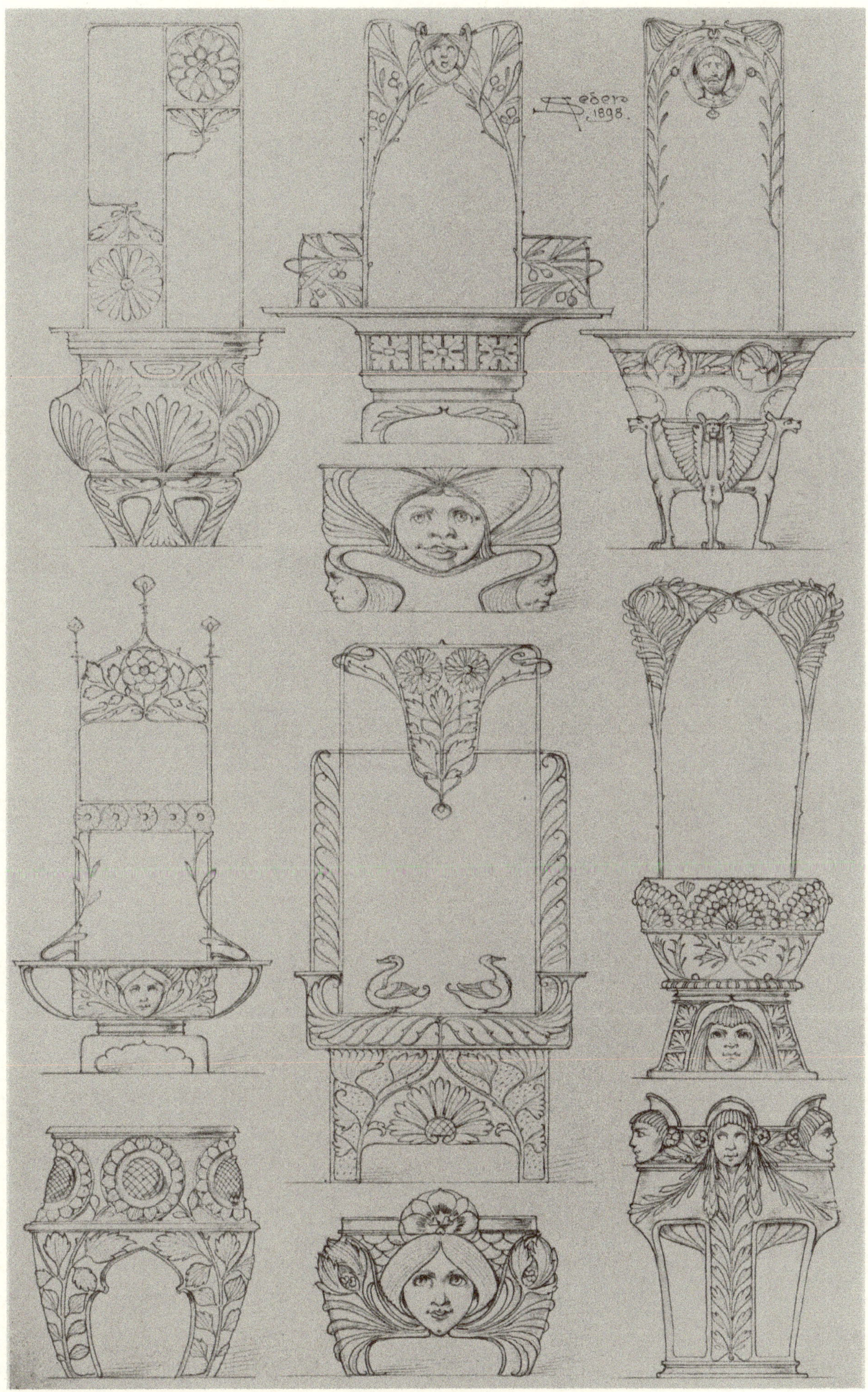
1898.

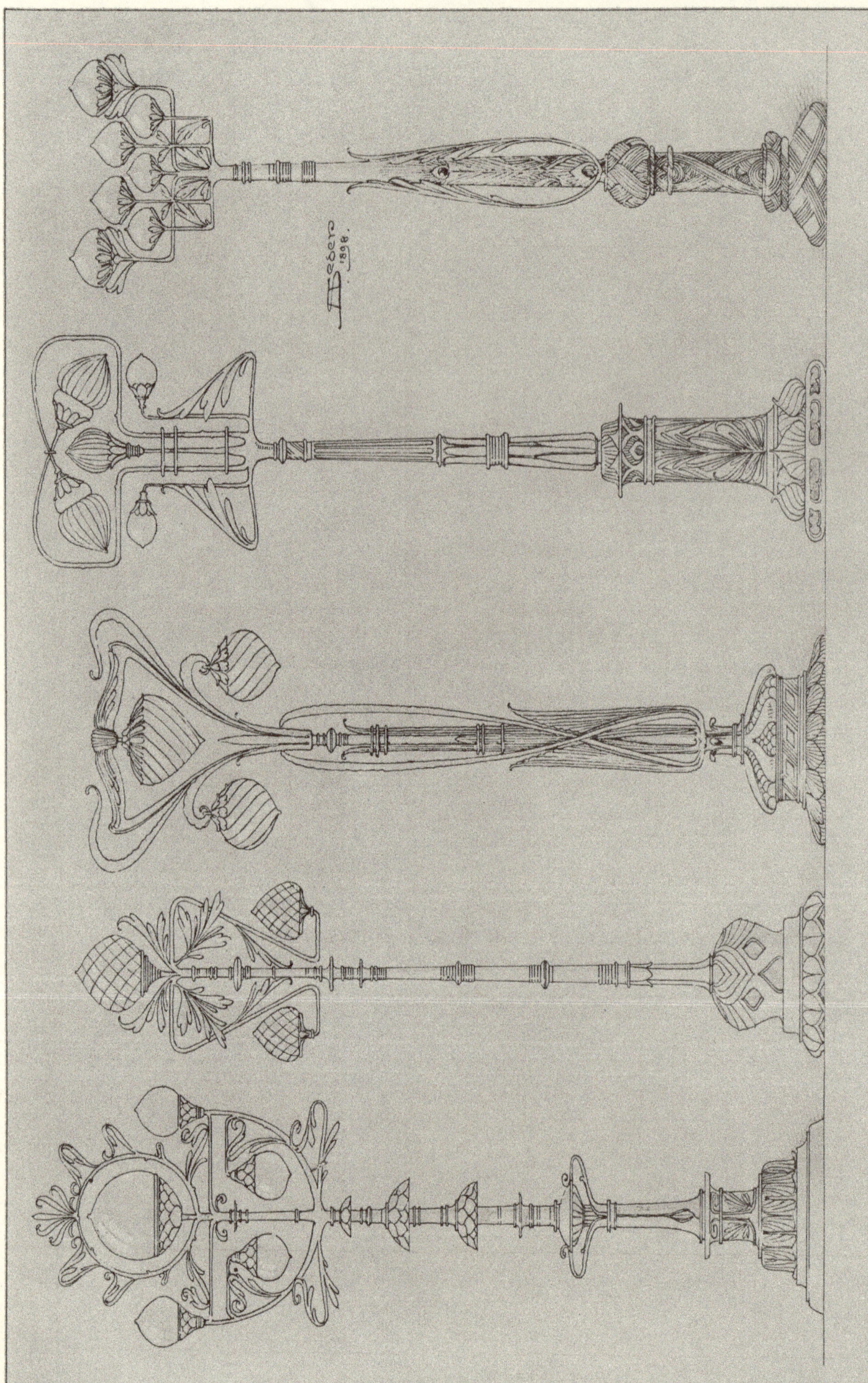

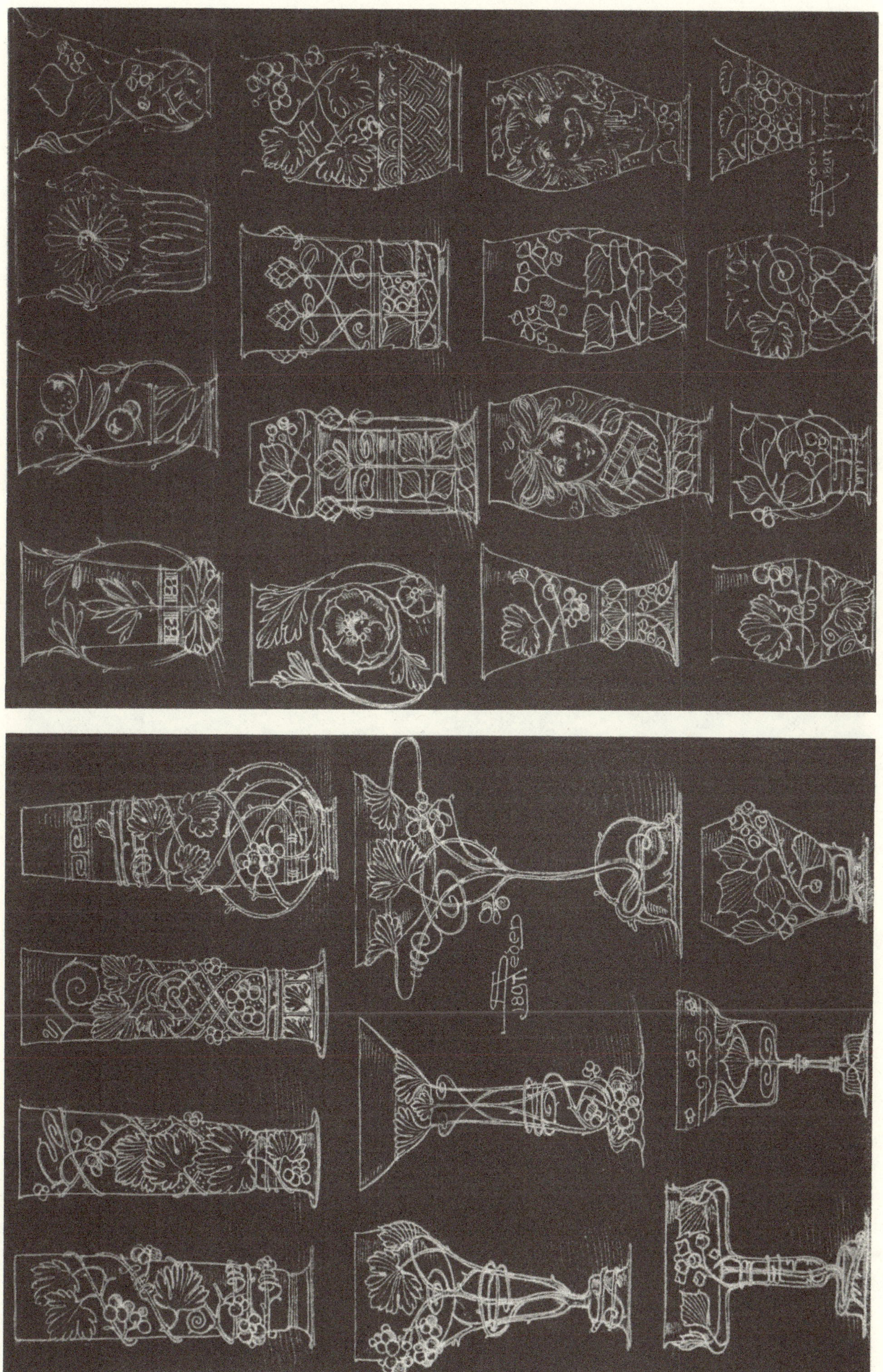

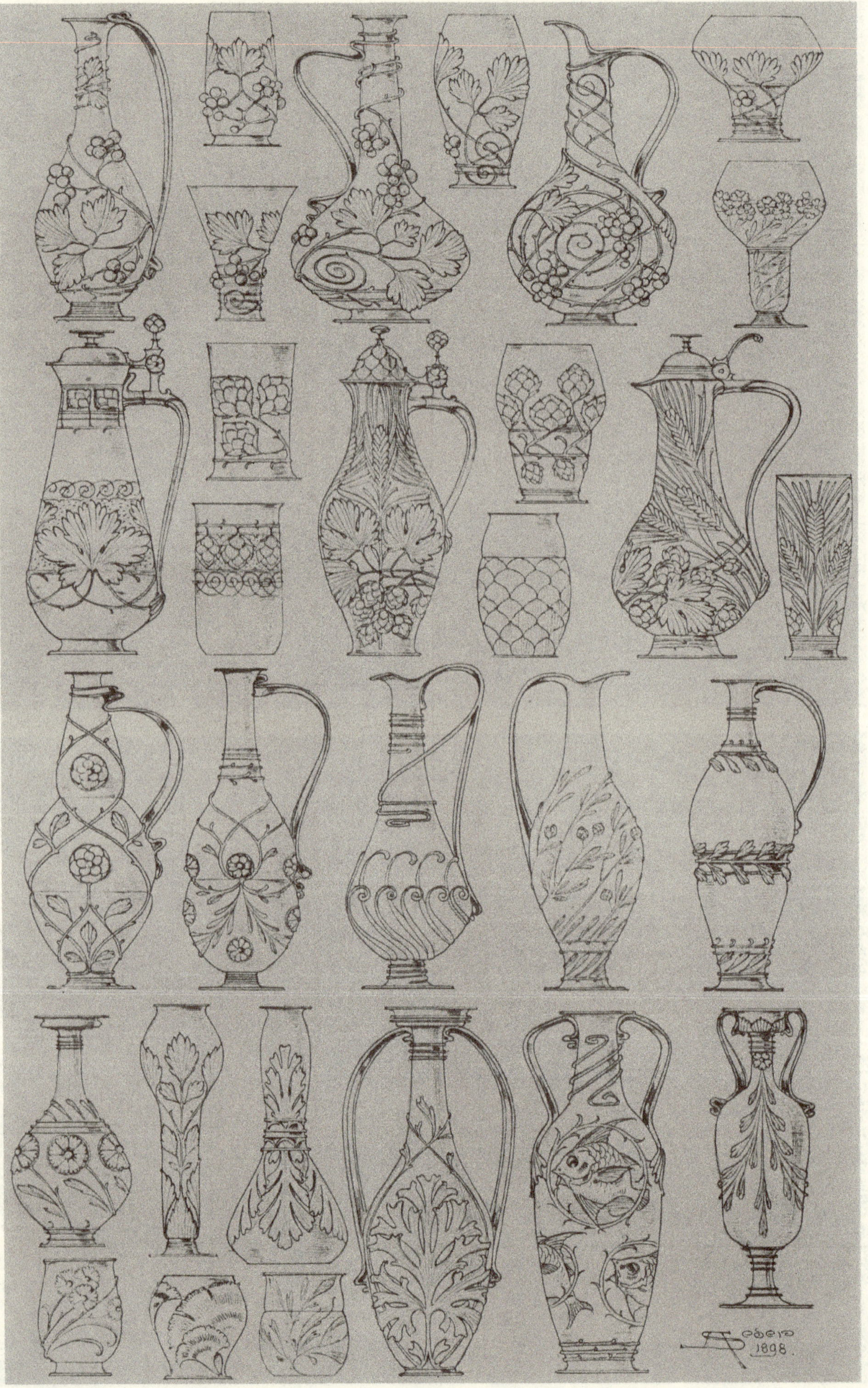
1898

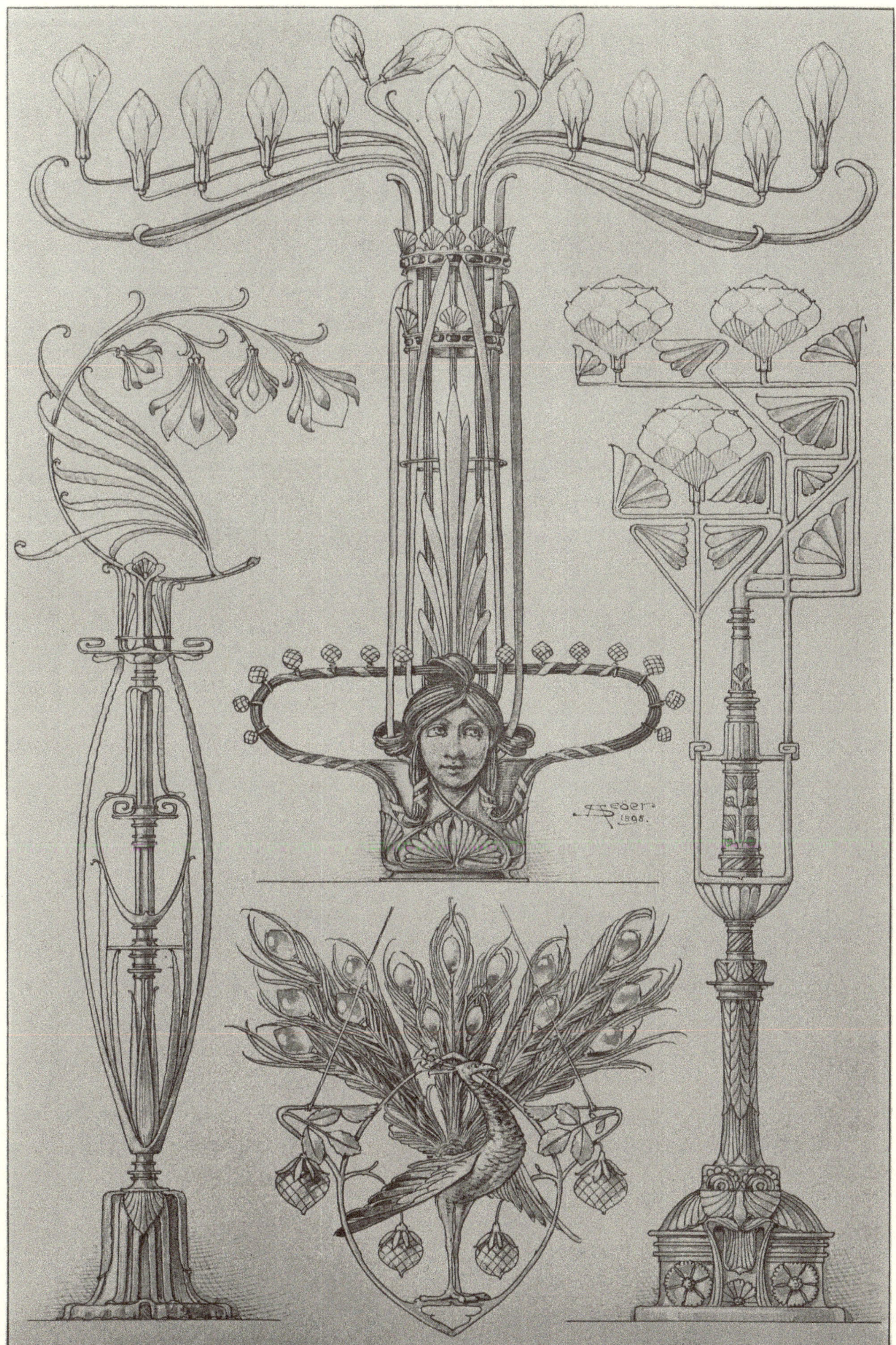
Seder.
1898.

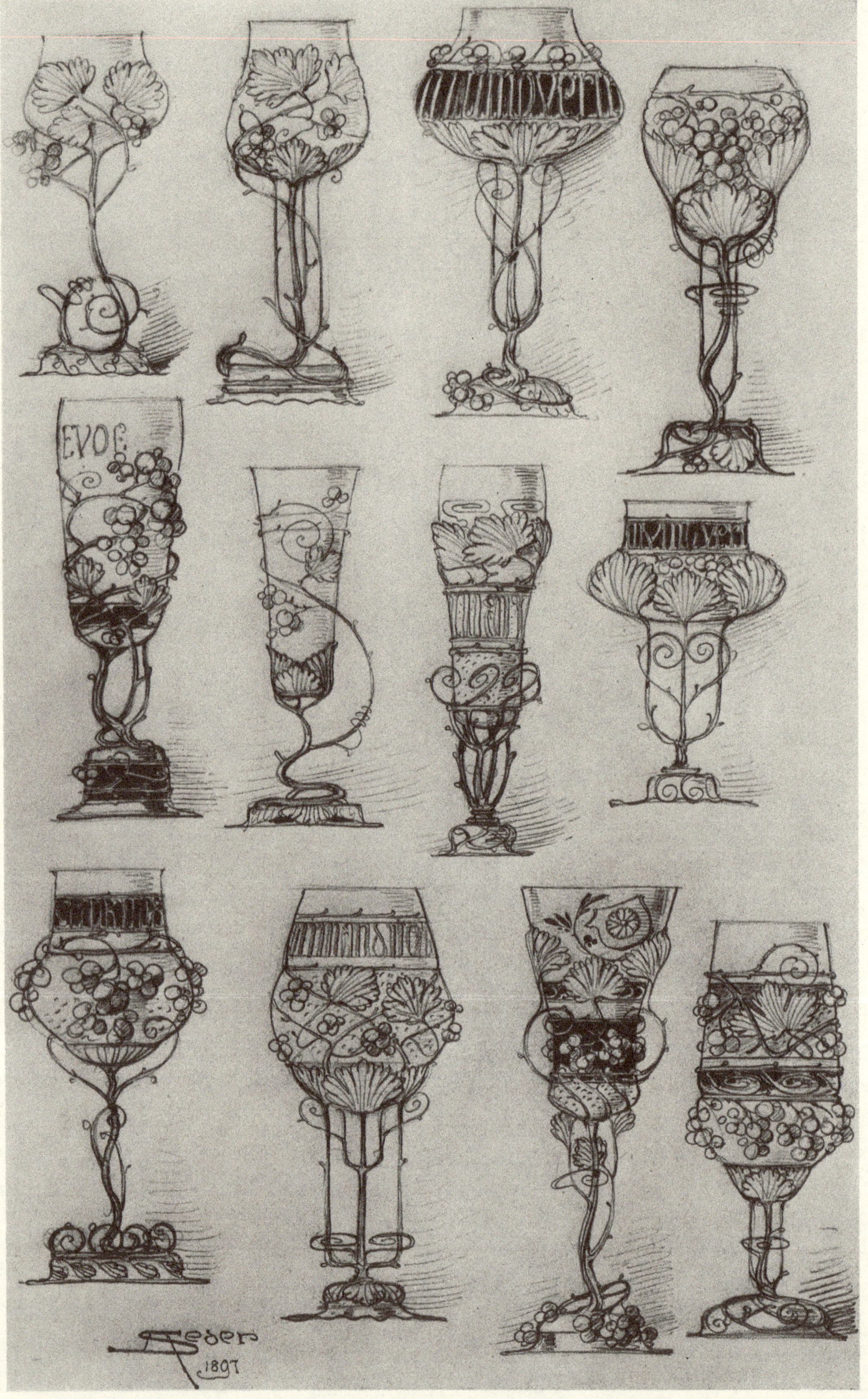
EVOE
Seder
1897

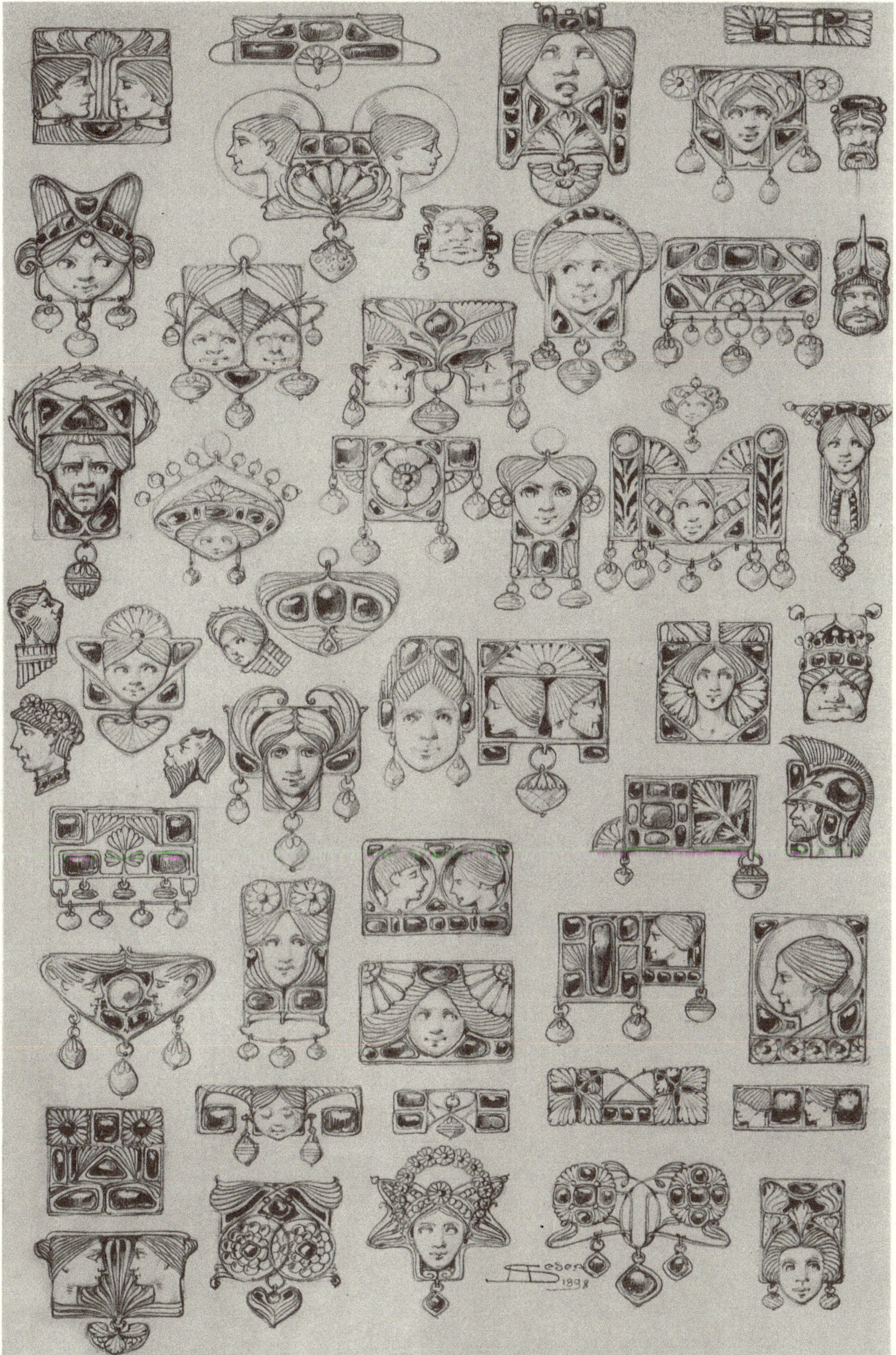
1898

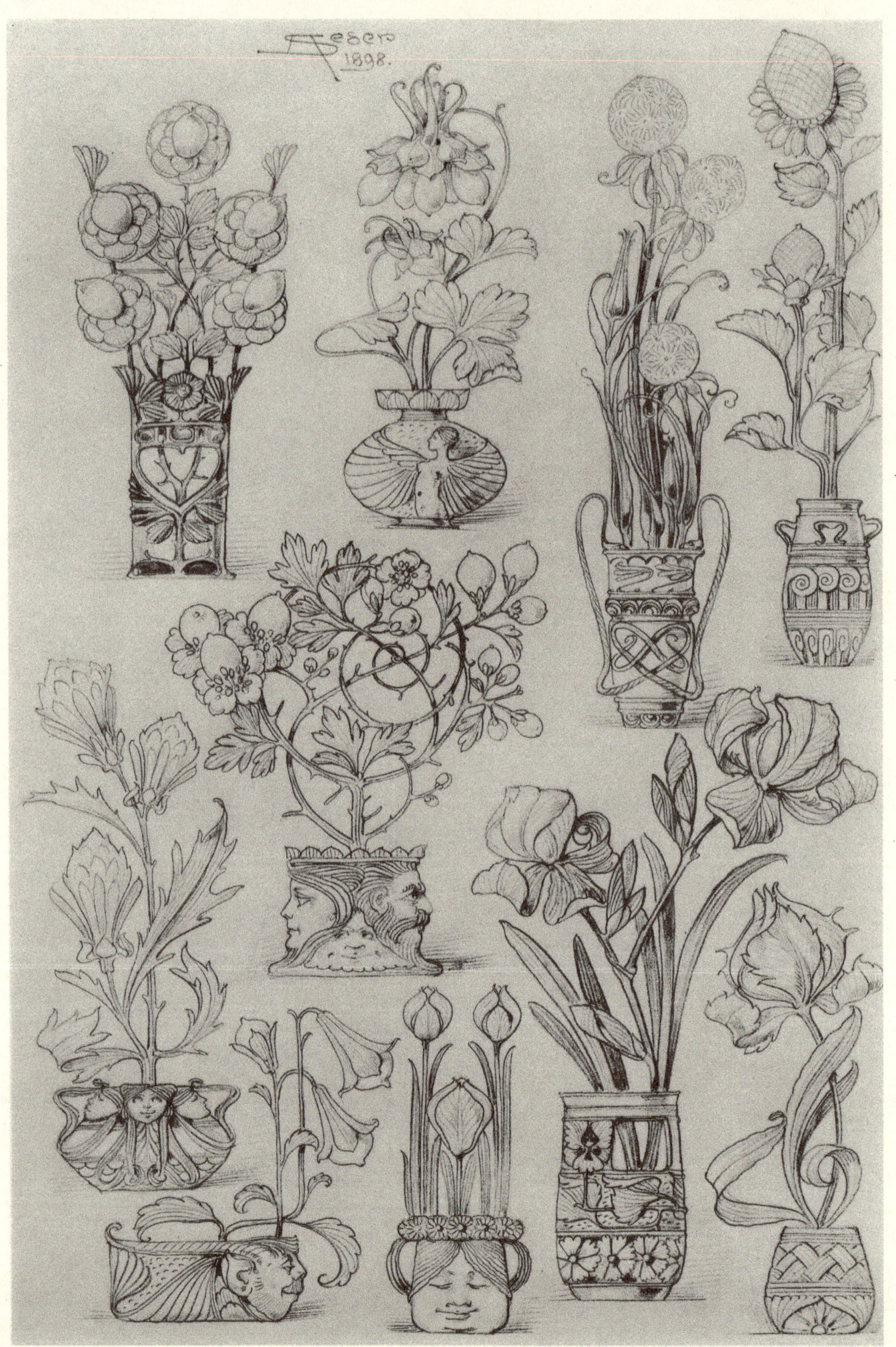
Seder
1898.

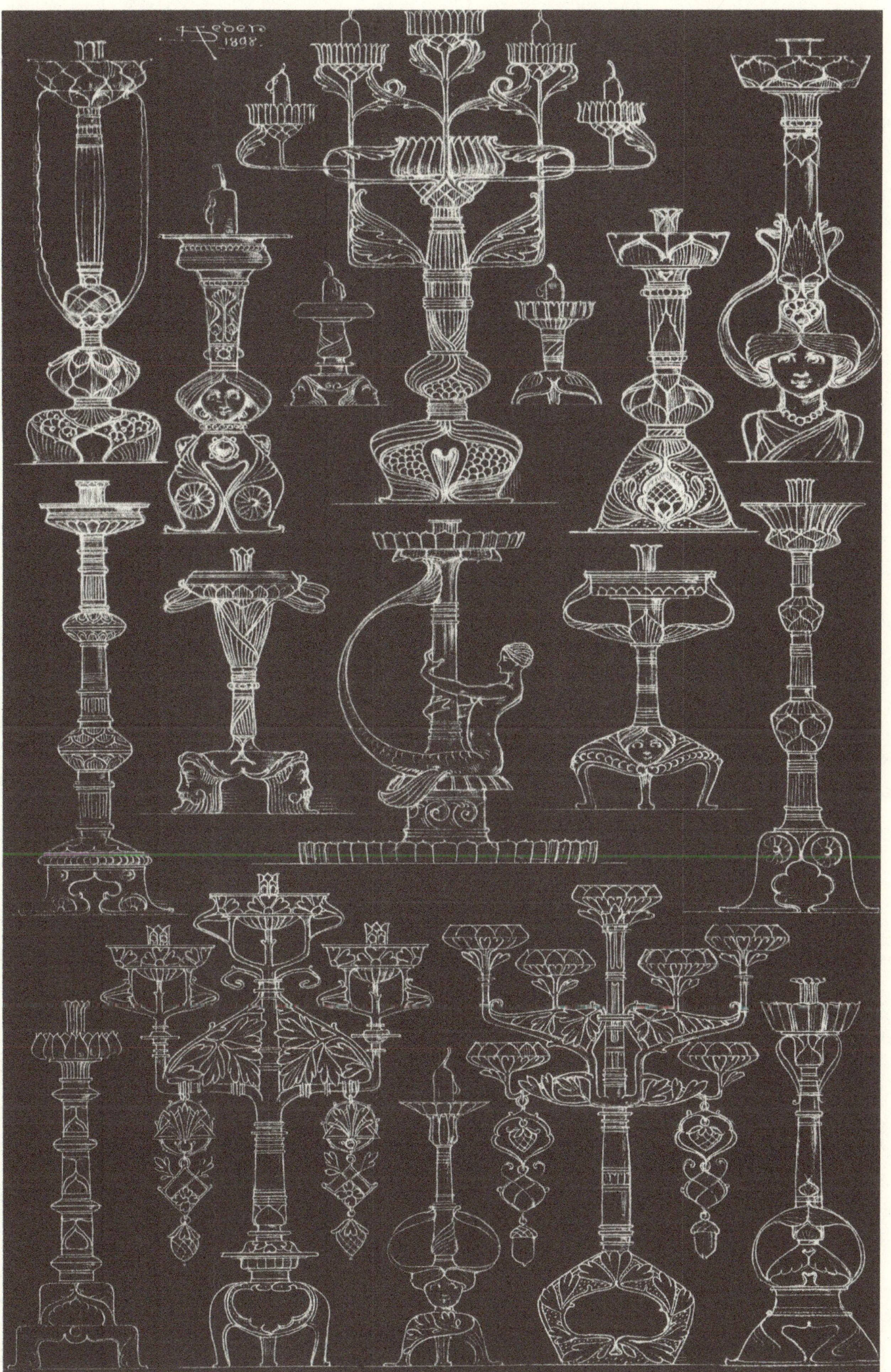
1898

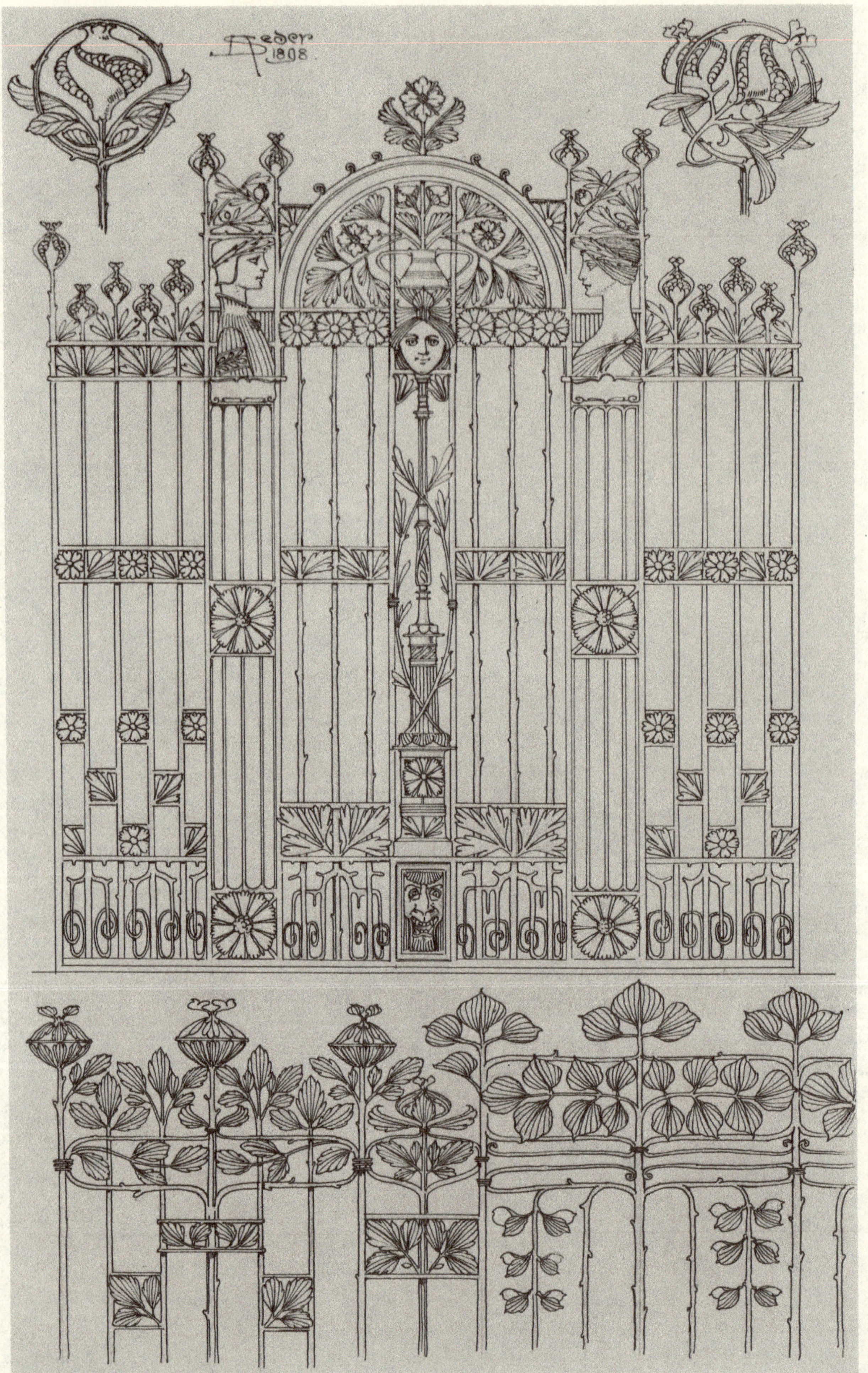

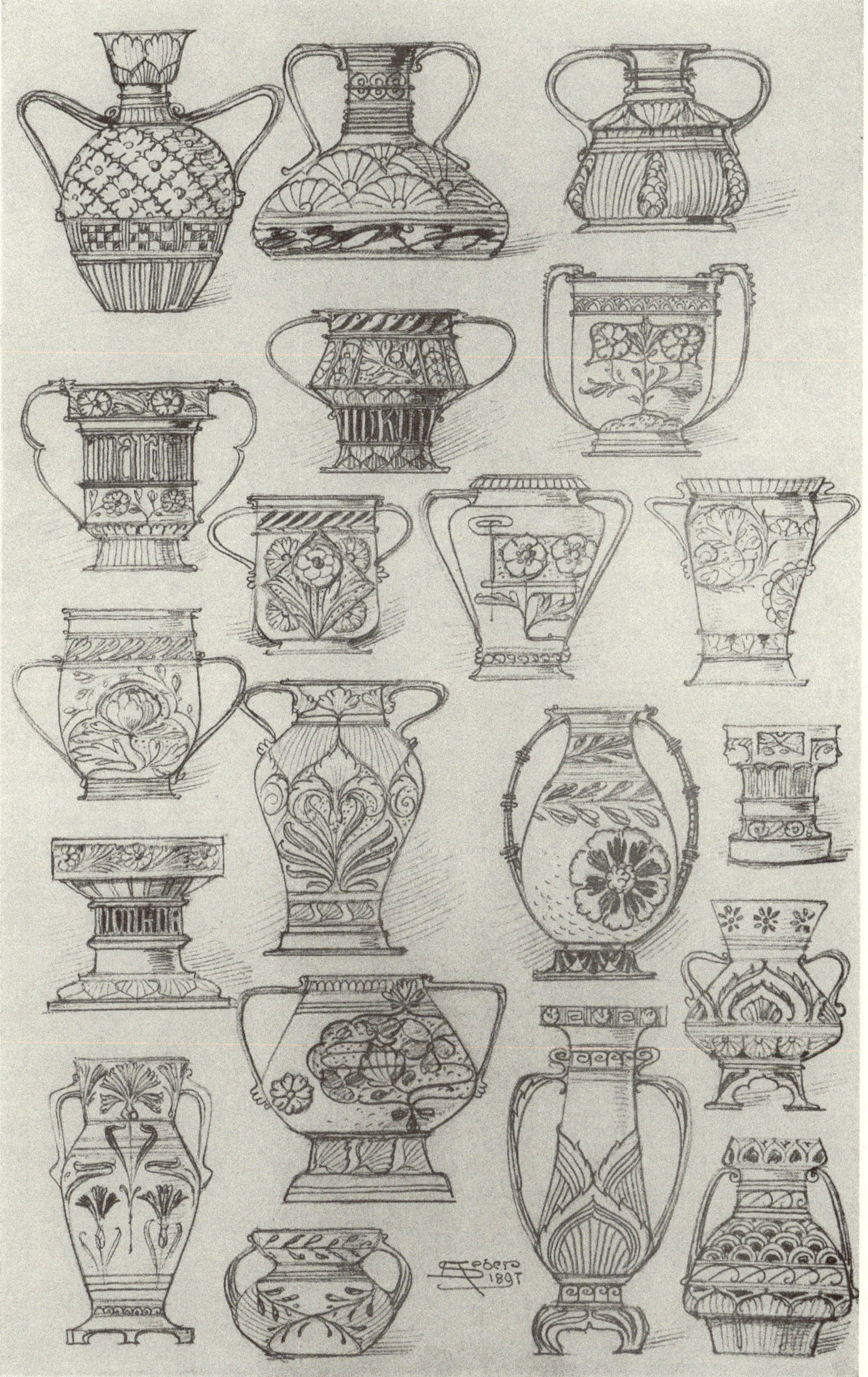
1897

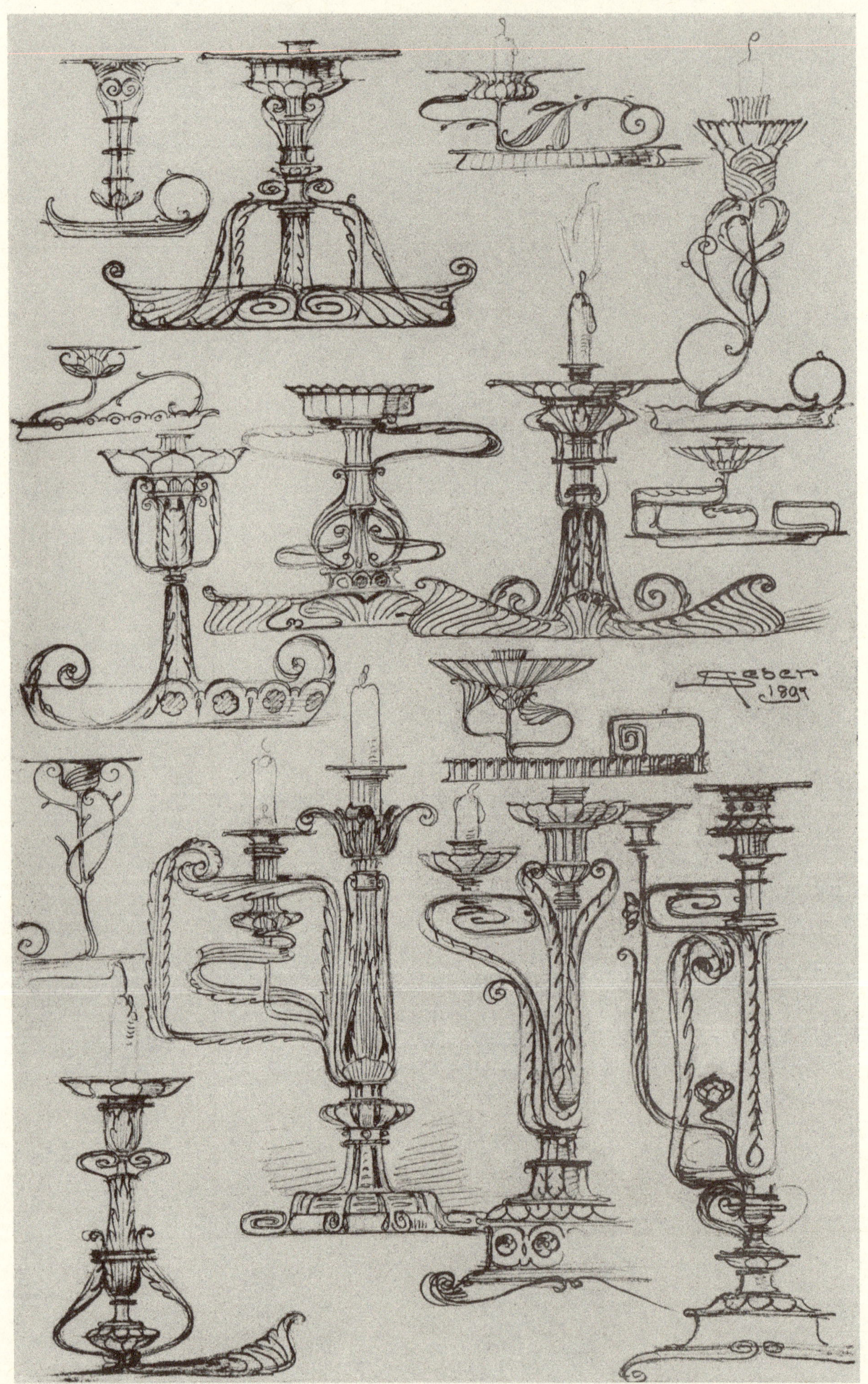
1897

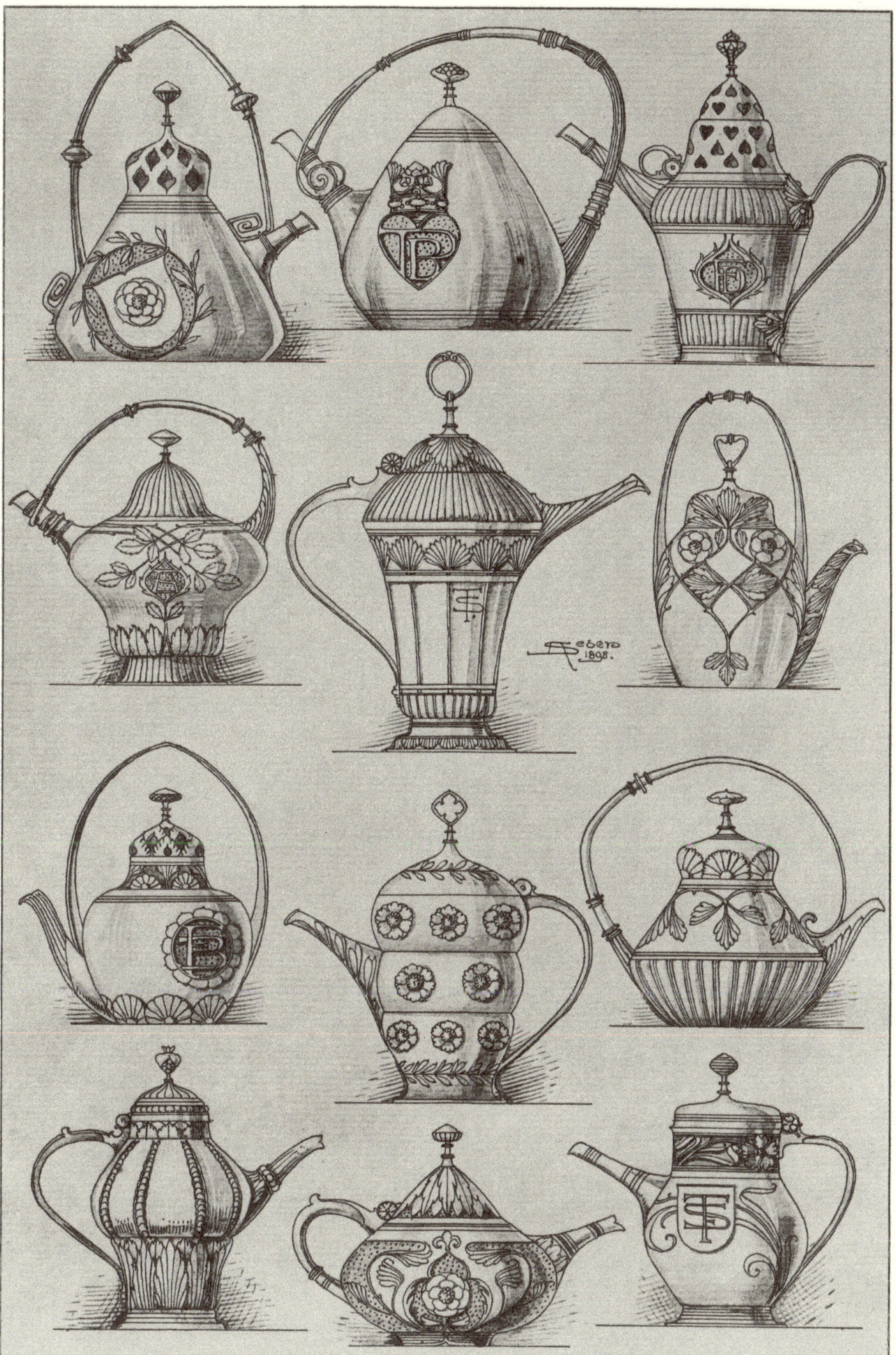
1898.

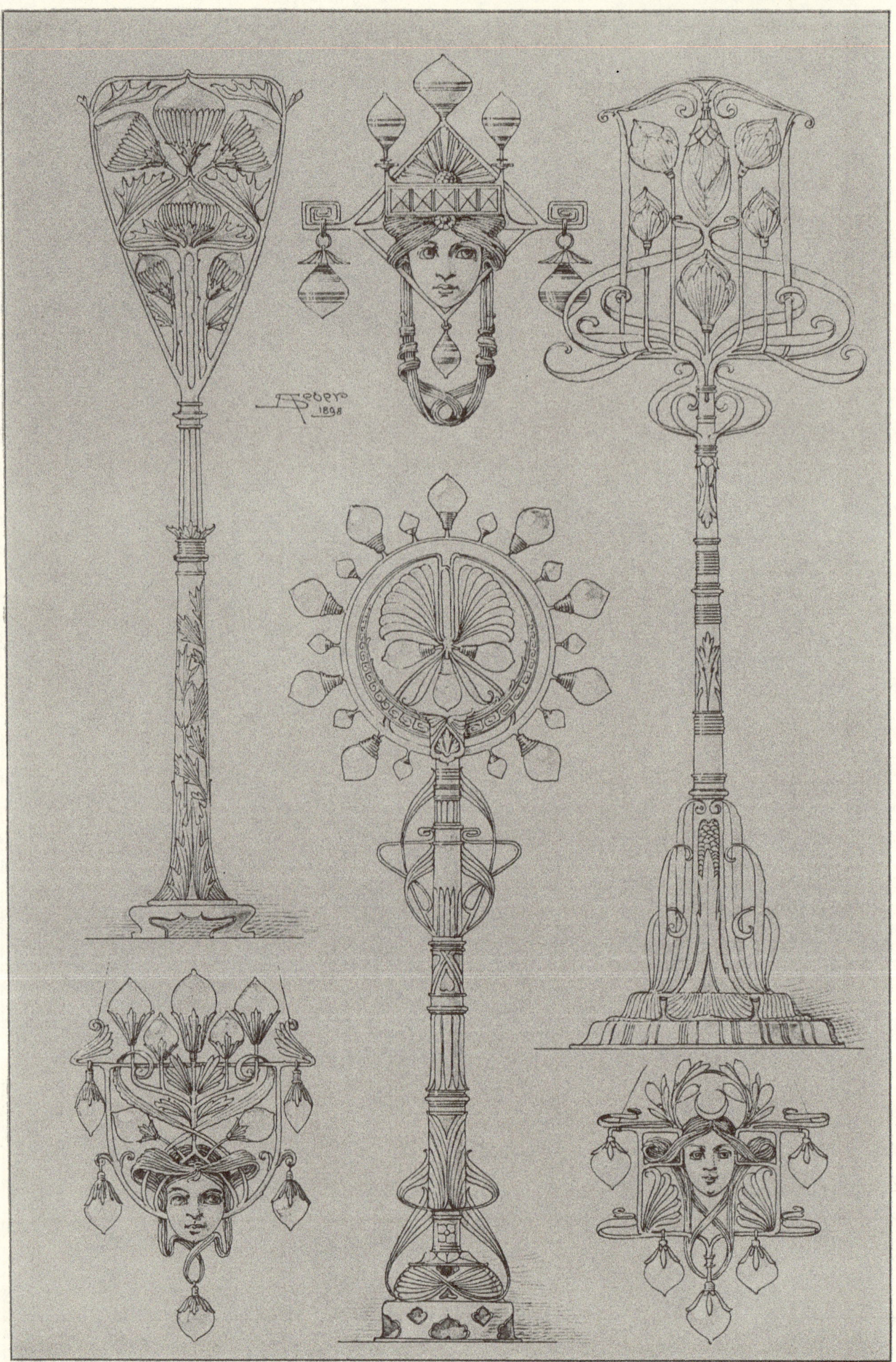
1898

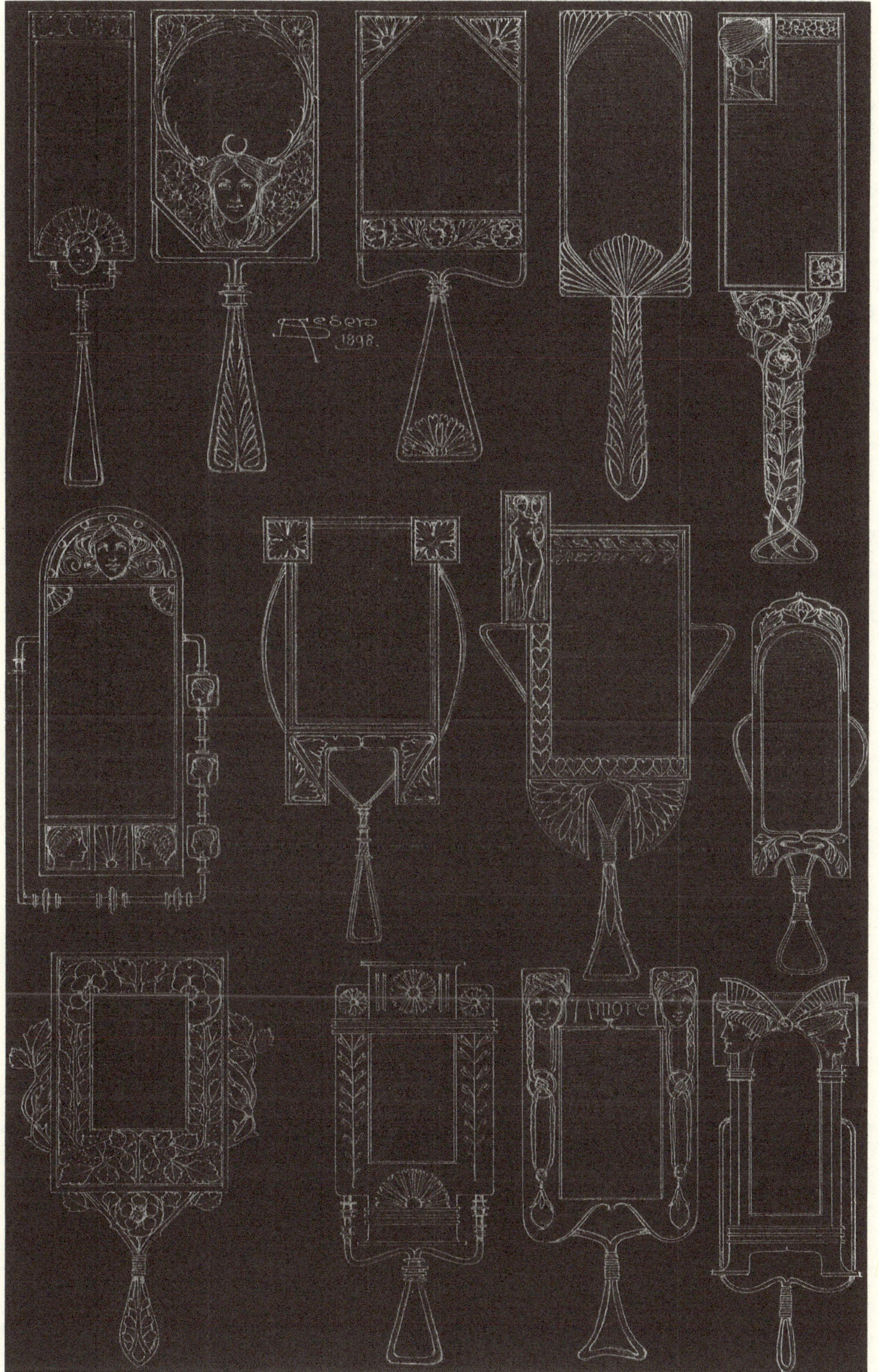
1898.
Amore

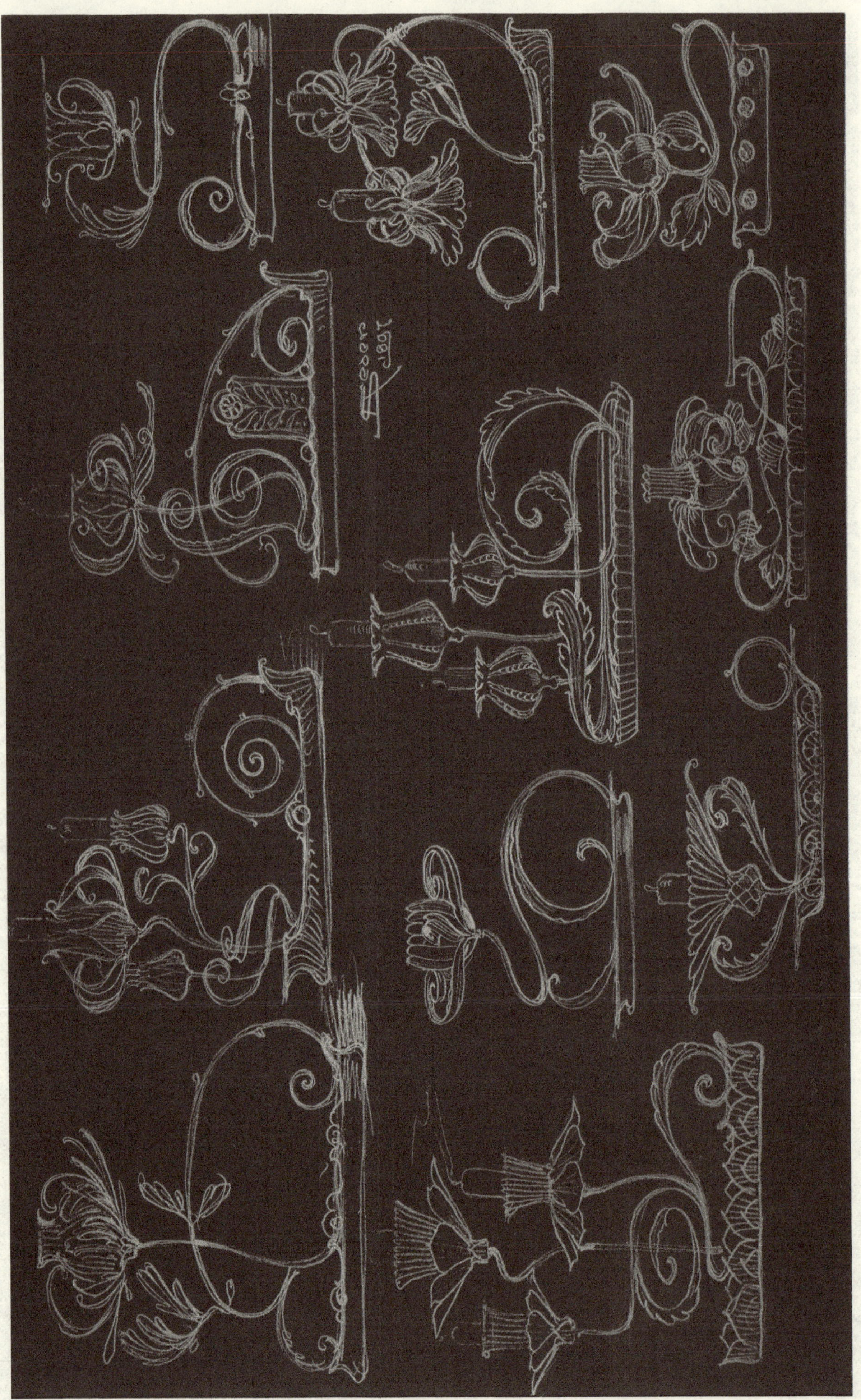

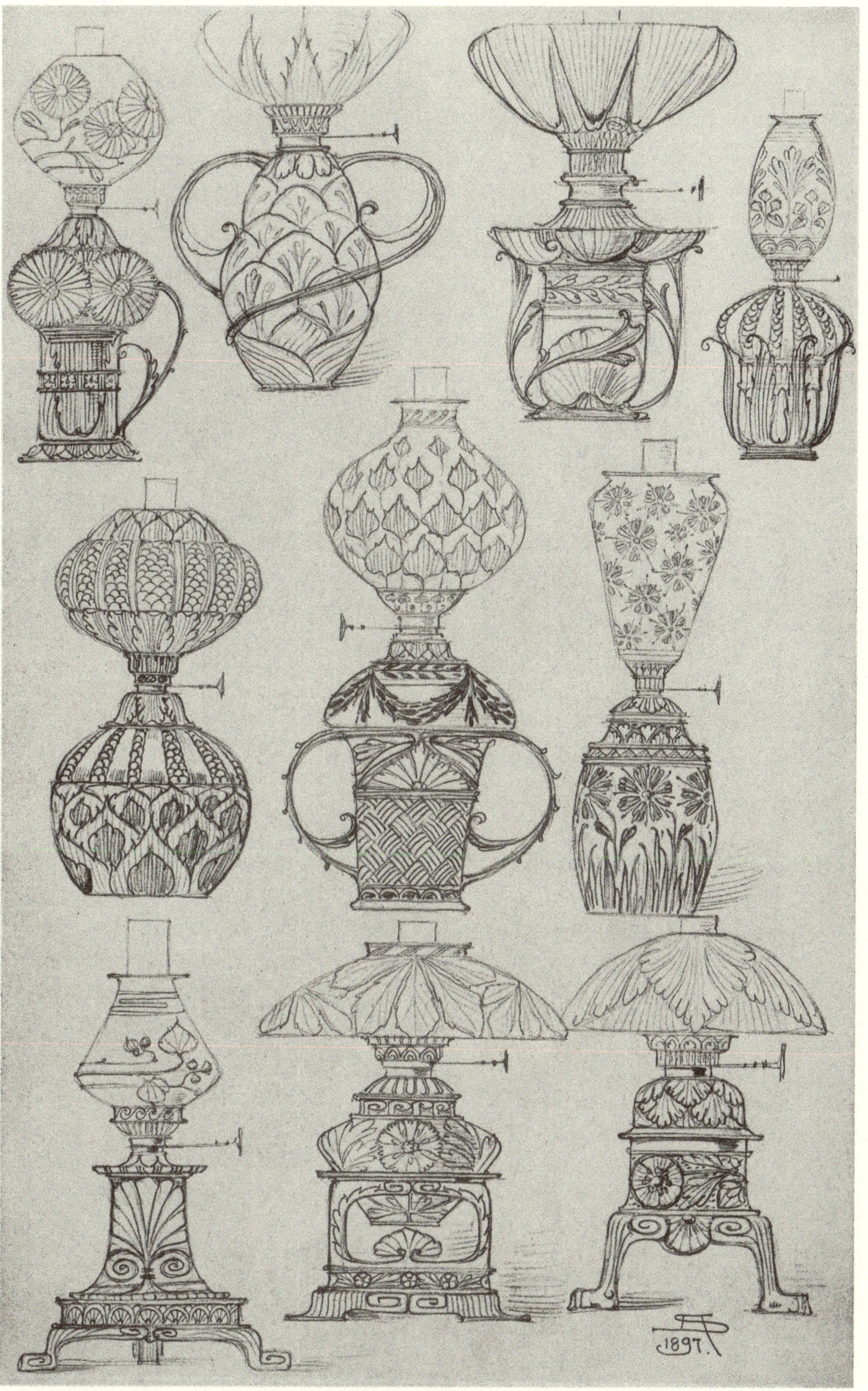
1897.

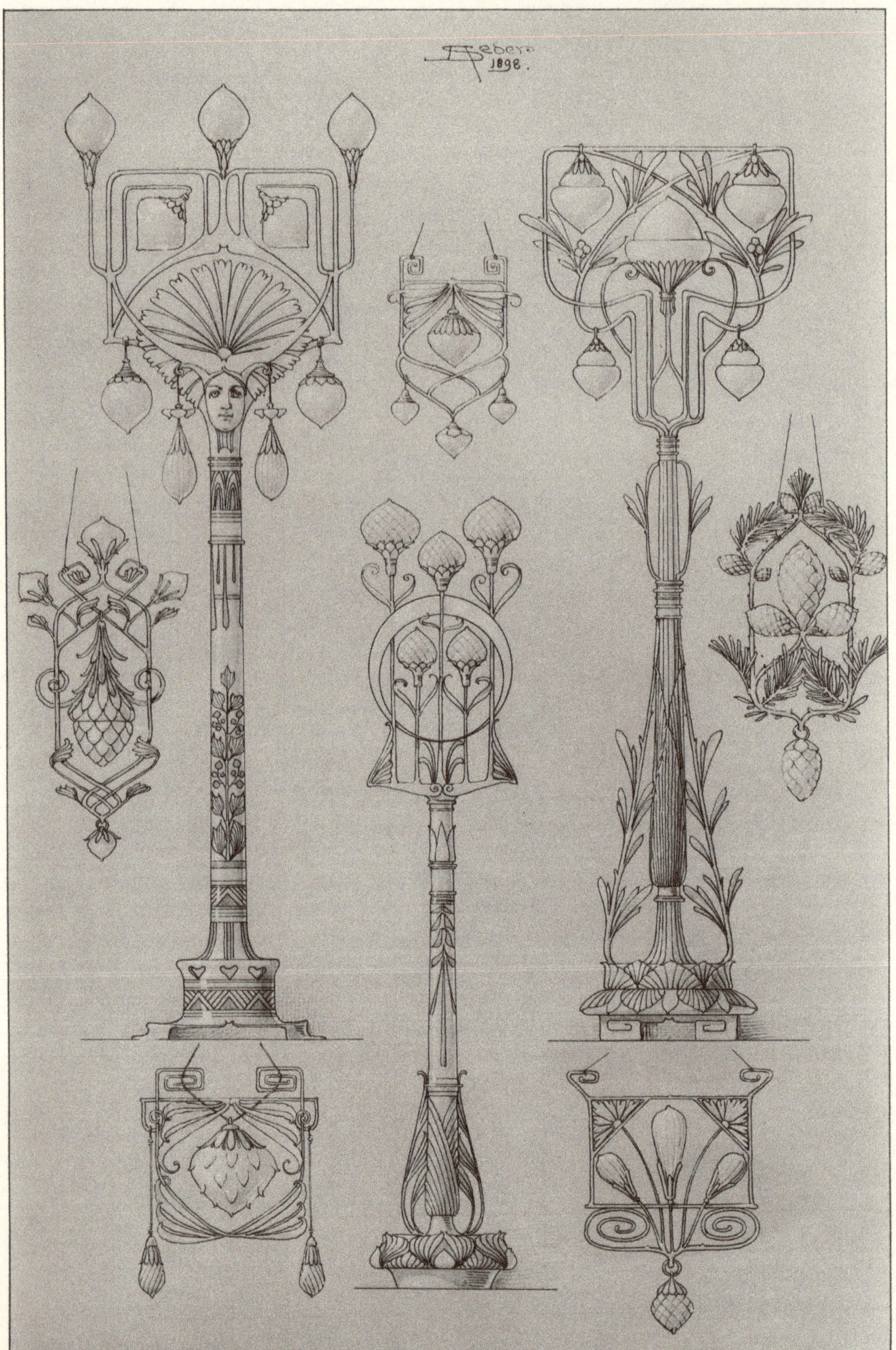
1898.